Facade Stories

Changing Faces of Main Street
Storefronts
and How To Care for Them

RONALD LEE FLEMING

A Publication of
THE TOWNSCAPE INSTITUTE, INC., Cambridge, MA 02138
and
HASTINGS HOUSE PUBLISHERS
New York 10016

D1409940

Photographs on cover (left to right, starting top left)
Renata von Tscharner/Renata von Tscharner/Renata von Tscharner/Ron Gordon/Renata von Tscharner/Kim Pulisti/Ronald Lee Fleming/Balthazar Korab, courtesy of William Kessler & Assoc., Inc./Renata von Tscharner/Steve T. Baird/Terry Schoonhoven/Renata von Tscharner.

Cover design: Renata von Tscharner

Library of Congress Catalog in Publication Data

Fleming, Ronald Lee.   Facade stories.

  Bibliography: p.
  Includes Index.
  1. Buildings—United States—Conservation and
restoration.   2. Architecture—United States—
Conservation and restoration.   I. Title.
TH3401.F54 1982   725′.028′8   82-11907
ISBN 0-8038-2398-3 (pbk.)

Published simultaneously in Canada by Saunders of Toronto, Ltd.
Don Mills, Ontario
Designed by Al Lichtenberg
Printed in the United States of America

Contents

This book is dedicated to my parents
Mr. and Mrs. Ree Overton Fleming

with special appreciation to
William I. Koch
Dover, Massachusetts

About the Townscape Institute

The Townscape Institute is a nonprofit, public interest organization in Cambridge, Massachusetts concerned with increasing the livability of cities, towns, and neighborhoods through conservation and enhancement of the built environment. The institute acknowledges the human need for connection and identity with place, a relationship that enriches the spirit and heightens one's sense of aesthetic pleasure. The founders conceive of the organization as a vehicle for carrying out innovative projects—in environmental education, townscape design, cultural planning, advocacy, and environmental art—that synthesize their own experiences in these areas over the past ten years.

More recently, Townscape has initiated a publishing program. The group's first book was *Place Makers: Public Art That Tells You Where You Are* (New York: Hastings House, 1981), co-authored by Ronald Lee Fleming and Renata von Tscharner. Place makers are works of public art and design that capture or reinforce the unique character of a site or space. The book presents case studies from across the United States—of sculptures, murals, fountains, pavement inserts, and street furniture. In the often bleak urban landscape of concrete slabs and mirrored glass, in anonymous plazas, malls, and squares, place makers provide a human scale, restore a much needed sense of connection, and sometimes add a touch of humor.

As that book suggests, the authors are particularly concerned with a broader public accessibility to the meanings and uses of place. To that end, the Townscape Institute has developed techniques for compiling an "environmental profile" that assesses the changing physical condition of places over time—their folklore, history, artistic traditions, resources, and contextual design constraints. This profile, usually elicited out of intensive work sessions with local people, becomes a basis for developing design ideas and themes that respond to the special qualities of a particular place. Artists and artisans then creatively translate such a profile into environmental art and design. Working with arts commissions, preservation organizations, and planning and redevelopment groups around the country, Townscape seeks to initiate or renew the sense of conection to place that can be a source of *civitas*—a bonding between people and the environment that is ultimately the basis of a community ethic.

In Cambridge, this concern encouraged Townscape to initiate a project with the Peabody Museum's Institute of Conservation Archaeology to undertake jointly the development of subway exhibitions that celebrate place identity. Entitled "History on the Line" and funded by the National Endowment for the Humanities, the exhibition will use archaeological artifacts, photographs, and text in the subway stations to interpret the changing condition of the places around them. It should complement the nationally recognized "Arts on the Line" project that Ronald Lee Fleming initiated as chairman of the Cambridge Arts Council.

In another project, the Bench and Bar Task Force commissioned Townscape to prepare a design strategy plan for Pemberton Square, a plaza in front of Boston's Suffolk County Courthouse, that will relate this space to the lives of five great Massachusetts jurists. The challenge there is to combine many different elements, such as bas-reliefs, interpretive panels, pavement inserts, and sculpture, to transform the impact of what is now a bleak space. At Boston's Logan Airport, Townscape staff employed the "environmental profile" technique to define the context for a mural celebrating the changing character of the airport from Quonset hut to concrete colossus. In New Orleans, the mayor secured Townscape's assistance in interpreting the cultural significance of Treme, a largely black neighborhood that is the traditional stamping ground of many early jazz musicians. It is an intriguing project because the interpretive panels are slated for columns of the elevated freeway that now divides what used to be the oak-lined grand avenue through the district. In a much newer environment, the rodeo-centered town of Davie, Florida, where rural pasturage is disappearing in the sprawl of Fort Lauderdale's exurbia, Townscape worked with a local engineering firm to devise a place making strategy and visual guidelines for a nascent commercial strip. The opportunity is to utilize public art and landscape elements at a highway scale. More recently the Architectural Heritage Foundation, owners of the Old City Hall building on Boston's School Street—a precedent-setting early rehabilitation—have asked the Townscape Institute to develop an interpretive program for the interior which incorporates the recent history of the rehabilitation, as well as a place-making strategy for the courtyard and the adjacent Freedom Trail using street furniture and public art.

Townscape's most recent publication is *On Common Ground: Caring for Shared Land from Town Common to Urban Park* (Harvard Common Press, 1982), a comprehensive study of commonly-owned land in America. *On Common Ground* traces the evolution of common land both in England and this country, offering design and maintenance guidelines for urban space and illustrating them with vignettes and case studies. The book concludes with a discussion of new applications of the concept of a common—a space for which a community shares proprietary benefits and responsibilities—and looks at examples across the country, ranging from an urban community garden in Brooklyn managed by a neighborhood group to a regional park in Oakland, California supported by corporate donations. With funding from the National Endowment for the Arts, *On Common Ground* will be the subject of a traveling exhibit to museums across the country in the fall of 1982.

Acknowledgments

Like some of the façades which we examine here, the information which comprises this book developed incrementally. The resource base for the stories included storekeepers and owners, developers and architects, historical societies and preservation commissions, and travelers with discerning eyes who helped me to find and then reconstruct what had happened to particular façades across the United States. There is no way that I can acknowledge them all in the front or weigh their relative merit, which often shifted as the stories developed and sometimes changed focus as I observed them over a period of three years. Instead, I have chosen to list the names of the contributors alphabetically in the back, hoping that I have recorded them all, but knowing inevitably that I have probably not, and asking them to please accept my gratitude for long distance telephone calls, meticulous correspondence about details of building renovation, and for the tediousness of having photographs reproduced. The revelation of the façade stories and their development over time was also a measure of the amount of good will which can be elicited for such a project as this, and for it I am profoundly grateful.

There are a number of people and institutions who helped to make *Façade Stories* a feasible project and gradually a reality. First my wife, Renata von Tscharner-Fleming, whose unstinting support, both emotional and logistical, enabled me to carry out the research and writing. Renata is an architect and principal of the Townscape Institute. My parents, the late Ree Overton Fleming, and Elizabeth Ebner Fleming, now of Laguna Hills, California, to whom this book is dedicated, have appreciated the vagaries of running an unendowed public interest organization and have contributed financial and logistical support. They nourished my early interest in historic preservation by spending their own vacation time following the ghost town trails that I suggested as a young enthusiast.

We owe a debt of gratitude to our board of directors and advisors, who understand the ethical basis for this mission, and have offered counsel and support. The board includes Philip H. Behr of Philadelphia, director of an investment organization; Roger Webb of Boston, president of the Architectural Heritage Corporation, which restored the Old City Hall; and Edmund H. Kellogg, Esq. of Pomfret, Vermont, a law professor. Our board of advisers includes David Bird of Cambridge, an indefatigable philanthropist and analyst; Lester Glenn Fant III, Esq., a lawyer in Washington, D.C., Eduard Sekler, Professor of Architecture and Visual Studies at Harvard University, and Dr. Charles G. K. Warner, also of Cambridge, whose insights, have been of particular value in charting the course of our work.

I am in addition grateful to friends who have hosted our trips in search of facade stories and other phenomena. These genial hosts include Grant and Ilse Jones of the urban design firm of Jones and Jones, Seattle; Dr. Richard H. Howland of Washington, D.C.; Pope and Constance Coleman of Cincinnati; Peter and Younghi Epstein of San Francisco; and Carole and Richard Rifkind of New York.

This book and the related activities of the Townscape Institue, have depended upon the financial assistance of individuals and foundations. I am particularly grateful for the early assistance from my friend, Robert Sincerbaux, director of the Cecil Howard Foundation, of Woodstock, Vermont, who underwrote the research in the fall and winter of 1979–1980. I am also very grateful to Henry J. Heinz II, Charles Muller, and Ann Roberts of New York, who helped us to secure funds from the foundations with which they are affiliated or provided us with direct support. This project was ultimately brought to fruition through the generous financial support of William Koch of Dover, Massachusetts, who provided a basis for final research and revision. We are very grateful to him and to Joan Granlund of Dover, who acted decisively to support this book and *On Common Ground*.

During the long course of this project The Townscape Institute staff have successively carried the brunt of the research and preliminary writing. They have included Penelope Simpson, a Smith College intern; Sara Williams, on leave from Brown University; Matthew Rutenberg, and more recently Lauri Halderman, who did much rewriting of individual stories. We give special recognition to Noré V. Winter of Boulder, Colorado, an architect who served as townscape director here at Two Hubbard Park. Mr. Winter identified several stories which we followed up here, and in addition drafted three of the western stories. He contributed significantly to the appendix, which he initially drafted and which is partially illustrated with his photographs. Ronald T. Reed, Townscape's architect did the final drawings based on Mr. Winter's ideas. Jonathan Propp has assisted in the final throes of pulling the manuscript together. My friends, author Brent Brolin and architectural historian J. A. Chewning, reviewed the introduction and made helpful suggestions. I am grateful to all of these people for their assistance over the three years of research and review as the book has developed.

We hope that all of these human efforts—the incremental research of the staff here in Cambridge and our collaborators across the country—will animate these façade faces, and will reveal the different facets of their presence. For it is a holistic view which we seek, one that comprises architectural history, design analysis, the saga of urban development, and even portraits of mercantile triumph and change. If we imagine them as a collocation of faces in one streetscape of the mind, they become both protagonists in the drama of the changing American streetscape as well as a chorus chanting for the broader realization of an ethic which can insure their survival.

Foreword

Facade stories loom up out of the memories of my childhood. I recall the first wooden false fronts of a ghost town which my father helped me to build on the land near our house in Los Angeles. We called this picturesque assemblage of wooden shacks a "ghost town" because it evoked with its main street, board walks, and hanging signs the old mining camps scattered around the west that I had seen on the excursions which I planned for my parents. In the simple wooden faces of these facades—signifying in my imagination—hotel, general store, sheriff's office—salvaged by my patient father from packing cases, I recreated a history I had only begun to comprehend. Like Tom Sawyer inveigling his friends to paint the fence, I succeeded in keeping a generation of neighborhood children gainfully employed as I choreographed the construction of my ghost town. I do recall now that despite the heavy landscaping of my parents' property, the buildings were not universally admired in the neighborhood; they required an annual inspection from the fire department and were eventually taken from me, as bulldozers cleared the land for a family house. This was a poignant experience in urban renewal for a young facade lover.

It was, nevertheless, the beginning of an educational process—the awakening of an interest in the built environment,—which would eventually take me on the journey of this publication. However, it took many years before I could see beyond my own imagination of the collected meanings of these "ghost town" facades, to some perception of the significance of facade design on Main Street America. Like most Americans I remained a visual illiterate until well through graduate school, able to identify historical styles and appreciate architectural monuments, but almost never looking closely above the street level at commercial buildings. Indeed, it was only after I had gone out of this country for a sabbatical year abroad, following service as an intelligence officer in Vietnam that I began to see facades. I sought some sol-

ace in the gentle English countryside, where I came across towns that were much remarked for the beauty of their composition. They were built all apiece, of the same materials, and their high streets reflected a harmony of craft and a compatibility of design, which was often maintained in today's more disparate world by careful design review of renovations. It was the civility of these streetscapes, the facades of their buildings keeping together, which caused me to look anew at Main Street America when I returned.

Though I understood that there was less agreement on forms in a pluralist society, and though I welcomed the vitality of America, which the sociologist Richard Sennett reminds us demonstrates the "uses of disorder," I was, nevertheless, appalled by the visual cacaphony of most main streets—the screaming out-of-scale signs pleading with the drivers of fast-moving automobiles to dismount for a loan, a soda or some Kodak film. My eyes were glazed by the bland and shiny new materials that sheathed handsome Victorian buildings and sought to make them just like the shopping centers on the outskirts which were depleting their trade. However, it was not until I viewed the mutilated facades of Victorian Saratoga that the scales fell off my eyes and I felt compelled to take some action in the defense of old facades and for the company—the cityscape—they kept.

Saratoga was a Victorian spa with an elegant main street, once lined with the sprightly figures of grand hotels, their porches festooned with gingerbread. I viewed it for the first time in 1971, and discovered that it had been sadly tarted up with behemoth signs and metallic new facade modernizations which covered the old dowagers like polyester. I learned that the Grand Union Hotel, once the premier hostelry on the street, had been replaced, despite last minute rehabilitation offers, by bumper space and a one-story Grand Union shopping center squatting behind it. I could only evoke this loss in my imagination, having never walked the long

galleries of the Grand Union Hotel, but it marked the beginning of my own modest efforts to alert people in other towns to the value of cityscapes, and particularly to the character of their building facades.

I saw in the chaos of the visual environment a metaphor. It was a metaphor of the failure of a cultural compact, a failure of different centers of power in our society to acknowledge a mutual sense of responsibility, which seemed to me at least one definition of what a "working" culture should do. Of course, the destruction or obfuscation of proud old facades is too simple a symbol for the larger failure of our society to come to grips with a national land use policy which could rejuvenate main street. However, mistreated facades do seem a poignant expression of a loss of accountability to a context—to a milieu—whether it is a business block or an entire downtown.

My own response to this problem was to form a public interest planning organization with offices in my house. I began lecturing about the visual environment and sending young teams of designers to work with main street merchants in towns along the eastern seaboard where planning efforts usually concentrated on the more abstract issues of land use plans to accommodate suburban sprawl and where the concept of townscape design—an effort to coordinate shapes, spaces, and textures along the street—was novel and initially had to be underwritten by foundation grants. We sought to create a new enhancement for main street perhaps somewhat akin to the "city beautiful" efforts of the 1890's. But it focused on the scale and character of main street amenities and facades rather than on the public monumentality, which distinguished the fragmented efforts of this earlier movement. Our projects depended upon the cooperation of individual merchants and property owners, and were necessarily incremental and, for the most part, low budget. The efforts were often cosmetic, but they were also sometimes dramatic, and did symbolize a reevaluation of main street—an acknowledgement of traditional character and rhythms.

Now, more than a decade later, it is clear we were, in fact, the pioneers in what has become a national concern for main street. Preservation groups around the country are rallying to it, conferences are convened about it on a regular basis, and more importantly, community development and economic development funds from the federal government were extensively used in the late 1970's to underwrite the facade design costs of downtown revitalization projects. With the recent cutbacks in funds local banks are filling the gap in some communities and the effort continues.

Some of the work which grew out of our early efforts is included in the appendix—"How To Improve Your Facade" section. These projects demonstrate the simplicity of many facade enhancement strategies, which acknowledge the original design. This is a fact which probably makes them less interesting to many architects, who would rather achieve their own "statement" with the construction of a new building or facade design and who do not want to endure the sometimes tedious logistics of financing collective main street improvements. But the book goes beyond the work I have personally directed and seeks to illustrate a variety of approaches to facade treatment across the nation. It comes at a time when architects, developers, planners, and preservationists are recognizing the need for more complex and varied solutions both for the revitilization of city centers and for the treatment of individual buildings. These are solutions that fit between demolition/new construction and totally faithful restoration.

The book tries to come to grips with this complexity, to identify a range of solutions, and judgementally, to indicate that some are better than others. It is on the whole, optimistic in tone, even as it recognizes that some of the best facade stories take place in the rubble of areas demolished for urban renewal. The particular qualities of these facades, their craftsmanship and visual interest, sometimes stayed the hand of demolishers, long enough for other forces to prevail in their regeneration.

Of course, *Facade Stories* takes cognizance of the enormous energy we possess in this country, for both good

Saratoga Springs, New York—"before and after" of Grand Union Hotel site.

The Grand Union Hotel, Saratoga, New York and the same site today after the building was demolished for a parking lot and Grand Union shopping center.

9

Paola, Kansas before and after. A dramatic change of identity, from Main Street menage to Butler Building monolith, one of the most comprehensive coverups in America still offers the redemption of a can opener. It is all there beneath the aluminum surface.

and ill effects on the urban environment. The sheathing in aluminum clapboard of the buildings around the courthouse square in Paola, Kansas, for example, an approach which we obviously discourage in the appendix of design advice, nevertheless represents a considerable, if misguided effort for improvement. It was a 1960's solution to modernizing downtown. A collective action for banality, but nevertheless a collective action that was an attempt to be public spirited. For such a unanimity of purpose would probably be difficult to achieve at a larger scale, where, conversely there might be less sense of community. *Facade Stories* should provide some context for evaluating this action rather than merely mocking it. By combining urban history, design analysis, and insights into mercantile aspirations in selected case studies, the book seeks to provide information in sufficient depth to encourage a more germane design solution than that which the merchants of Paoli imposed on themselves.

Facade Stories is the final volume in a trilogy which has absorbed some of the energies of The Townscape Institute during recent times, and it can be read in conjunction with our other recent books, which have appeared in the past nine months; *Place Makers: Public Art That Tells You Where You Are*, and *On Common Ground: Caring For Shared Land From Village Green to Urban Park*. Each focuses on an aspect of the built environment where, in our judgment, there are opportunities for more responsible public policy and private initiatives to create a more humane environment.

On Common Ground uses an exploratory study of New England greens and commons as a basis for evaluating how design and management strategies can be applied to stimulate a contemporary sense of proprietorship for public or quasi public space amongst corporations, foundations, and citizens' organizations. It recalls the analogue of the original proprietors who were responsible for the care of early New England commons as a means of examining how this concept can be applied to public spaces today. It demonstrates with case studies of recent parks across the country how the private sector can assume a role of proprietorship of public spaces at a time when public resources for care are shrinking.

Our other book, *Place Makers*, inventories public art and design elements which reveal, enrich, or reinforce a sense of connection to a place. It also defines a methodology for building up an informational profile about a site which can guide decision making about public art so that it encourages greater place meaning in the design approach. Now, this book *Facade Stories*, looks at an elemental aspect of the streetscape—fronts of buildings—in order to suggest by varied example, how these faces on the street can continue to serve the function of humanizing it—making us accountable to the street—and to each other. Seen as equal parts of a trilogy concerning an architectural typology—object, building, and place. We hope that these books will not only fortify by example the convictions of readers interested in sustaining an ethic for the built environment but will also encourage them to take action to more fully realize that ethic wherever they live and work. Ultimately this action can insure what should be the long term goal of a preservation program—to create a sense of value which can secure a past for what is built in the future.

Ronald Lee Fleming
Cambridge, Massachusetts
May 1982

A refurbished eagle symbolizes the reemergence of a facade in the center of Winooski.

10

Introduction

Dictionaries invariably give two definitions of the word facade: a side of a building receiving special architectural treatment, and also, a false, superficial, or artificial effect. A facade can be likened to a face, and it is indeed the face that a building presents to the street which often combines these two definitions.

Because a facade is likely to be different from, and more elaborate than, the building behind it, it is sometimes considered a deception, yet paradoxically, it is this very sense of artifice that supports its meaning on the street. For seen cheek by jowl with other facades comprising a streetscape, the face can help to sustain a larger integrity of form that transcends the artifice of its demeanor and registers a communal vision.

Even when viewed alone without this context of adjacent facades, it can reflect certain attitudes and proprieties which authenticate the aspirations and the values of a period. As the facade changes over time, its portals, signs, windows and ornamentation, become a convincing artifact documenting cultural change. On Main Street America, where most of the faces in this book are located we witness an evolution of facade designs that record a variety of attitudes and a panoply of periods.

Sometimes on the face of a single building we can view much of the story of its own Main Street. We can see the exuberant optimism of the 1890's in the elaborately detailed and robust forms of cornice and parapet, the fascination with the machine age in 1930's Deco bands of sleek carrara glass and stainless steel still sheathing the second floor; and the minimalist aesthetic of the 1960's aggregate panels or metal grilles hiding the first floor clerestory, and finally a homey touch for the 1970's, a mini–mansard first floor cornice cover, like an eye shade, trying to attract attention to an age of self expression. Many layers of artifice, perhaps, but with them some truths about our cultural condition.

Although some of the facades which we profile are now isolated from the cityscape, the traditional strength of commercial facades was their cohesion; standing adjacent to each other, block upon block, they formed the room of the street. They functioned both as backdrop or stage set to the street, viewing the drama on it, and also as a sort of chorus sounding their own rhythms, which often articulate the action of the street. In the past, the facades came carefully made up, formally attired; they summoned up their best manners and hoped to impress each other with a measure of pomp and circumstance. Often, in addressing themselves to comport with the street, the facades expressed a yearning for a

Facades on Broad Street, Richmond's principal commercial artery wear the costumes of several styles: Victorian Italianate, Classical revival, Art Deco, Art Moderne, Sixties and Seventies International Style derivatives and kitsch.

Facades on Liberty Street, Bath, New York 1965

11

Leone Battista Alberti's facade for Santa Maria Novella, Florence, Italy

Francesco Borromini's Sant Carlo alle Quattro Fontane, Rome

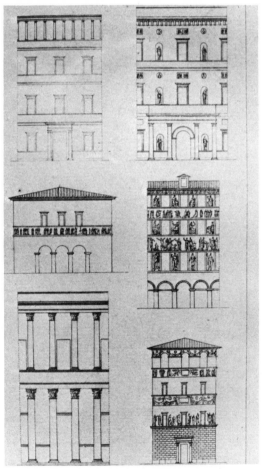

An illustration from J.N.L. Durand's book on facade design, *Précis des leçons d'architecture,* 1802

Charles Garnier's Paris Opera House demonstrates with a muscular heroicism how a facade can command a street. This is not deceptive grandeur; the interior staircase is as magnificent a stage setting as the exterior.

Marcus Cumming's pattern book, *Architecture,* supported his effort to set design standards for Troy, New York's, rebuilt facades, 1865.

12

The strong verticality of the Main Street with facades set flush against the sidewalk is evident on Kansas Avenue, Topeka, Kansas, 1876 when the town was barely twenty years old.

grander image than was in accord with the building behind them. They performed this function for centuries, creating both an illusion of their importance and a reality of civility. Their ordering arches, columns, cornices and decorative elements created a rhythm of behavior—a cityscape—which ultimately gave dignity to their pretensions.

The antiquity of the facade presence is well established. The Romans disguised the masonry vault construction of their public buildings by adopting the Greek architectural orders for their facades. Vitruvius, the Roman architect and engineer, set down the rules for appropriate use of these elements to achieve an ultimate propriety: "that perfection of style which comes when a work is authoritatively constructed on approved principles." Renaissance architects reinterpreting Vitruvius, strove for a noble effect. The architect and scholar Leon Alberti, who wrote his own interpretation of Vitruvius, attached a classical facade to the medieval Santa Maria Novella in Florence with a mathematical ordering of space in harmonic proportions which demonstrated the facade's potential for expressing grandeur. Such a goal led other architects quite logically to the exploitation of the facade's capacity for visual impact. As Renaissance expression grew more mannered this resulted

in facades such as Francesco Borromini's Sant Carlo alle Quattro Fontane in Rome, with its bulging volumetric planes in a compressed space.

Many 19th century facades in the commercial districts of cities followed in this tradition, incorporating grand references to the classical past as dictated by Beaux-Arts academicians such as J.N.L. Durand, whose *Precis des leçons d'architecture* was a primary teaching book of the period. Though the department stores, banks, and business blocks did not have the authority of Charles Garnier's Opera House in Paris, designed to overwhelm the viewer down a broad avenue, they did express a loftiness of purpose that could be structurally and ideologically separated from the buildings behind them. Classical design principles were applied to the ordinary commercial structures of the day as banks and dry goods stores pretended to be temples and palaces.

Using their own pattern books American architects created facade designs for specific building types. The new books responded to the industrial technology of cast iron cladding, rolled glass for larger window openings, and standardized parts which created a new verticality on the 19th century American Main Street. In the boom towns of the West, with their improvised false-fronts, the wooden facades were an af-

firmation of form over substance, and as they were replaced by the more permanent cast iron or brick and stone, there was an assertion of mercantile authority that transcended the confusion of a society in flux. They created a sort of disparate grandeur. The Portland Oregon waterfront anchored by the elegant phalanx of these cast iron fronts bore witness to such convictions—it survived until the next generation's riverside highway transformed the site of these sentiments into black top.

The presence of a classical revival which affected facades on Main Street and more important buildings of the

The false or enlarged fronts of many western boom towns like Georgetown, Colorado expressed a promise that never solidified into lasting prosperity.

13

Cast iron facades, Portland, Oregon constructed in the 1870's–80's were manufactured architecture based on classical motifs, replaced by a waterfront highway in 1940–1941.

mid 19th century gave rise to alternative views. The English critic, John Ruskin, with his appreciation of the Gothic style reprimanded his peers for facades that put on pretences about their function. Ruskin wrote in *The Seven Lamps of Architecture* in 1849, "That building will generally be noblest, which to the intelligent eye discovers the great secrets of its structure." The moral dimension to this writing which posited that the facade must express the functions of the building in order to be truthful about the values of society. Ruskin combined this moral assertion with a dictum about the honesty of materials, wanting only wood or masonry that would clearly indicate how the structure was put together. His words were an ironic precursor to the architectural canons of the International Style in the early twentieth century.

Apostles of this later period, Le Corbusier and Ozenfant, believed that a building acquired integrity by expressing its function clearly and they created buildings which used the new industrial materials with an often elegant simplicity that denied giving special importance to a facade. The designers of what became the Modern Movement viewed their buildings as three-dimensional objects in space, tending toward transparency and avoiding decorative references to the past that got in the way of primary associations with shape and materials. They deliberately refused to attach themselves to place and time; in other words, they wanted to be

truly international. But when their buildings were placed in the context of existing streetscape their calculated dissonance often gave offense, jarring the established rhythms of the existing facades. Brent Brolin has examined this problem in his critical study, *Architecture in Context:*

> Eschewing historical forms, modern architects then had no choice when it came to putting a new building next to an older one. They could not make a stylistic connection, so they had to "contrast" with the older structure . . .

Pietro Belluschi's International Style addition of 1945–46 to the old cast iron Ladd & Bush Branch of the U.S. National Bank was a sleek contrast. Belluschi said that no old iron was available at the time, and in a true modernist fashion did not want to "mimic" the old. Later, the bank found some cast iron elements, from their sister bank in Portland which had been demolished, and this earlier jewel of modernism was replaced by a more traditional annex in 1967. The original building was demolished as well and its old cast iron attached to a new interior. An interesting change of sensibilities.

obviously the potency of these contrasts decreases as their frequency increases; they make impact only when they are exceptional. Unfortunately they have become the rule. Our cities are peppered with them, and the result is chaos rather than drama.

In this way, the Modern Movement contributed to the decline of the facade as a supportive character in this drama of the streetscape.

The Victorian facades that form the principal stage set for so many American Main Streets often went through

Cable Piano became The Corley Company, jewelers, with restraint and decorum on Broad Street, Richmond, Virginia, about 1915.

cade patterning. The changes between these periods and our own time can be likened to the difference between a man adding a watch fob or donning a waistcoat to hiding his dress shirt under a new polyester leisure suit.

The more recent alterations in facades along Main Street try to respond to the need to be legible to the automobile and to emulate the competition in nearby shopping centers. The projecting signs have gotten larger and thicker—fat blimps of internally lit plastic—often destroying the delicate balance of the other facade elements. The facades themselves have been sheathed to mimic the simple forms of the shopping centers or to create contrast with homilies of kitsch hybrid: mansard, Olde English, western, and colonial. Neither approach enriches or draws upon the existing architecture or supports place meaning. Both are ahistorical, recognizing neither the antecedent of the facade design nor understanding its context in the streetscape, and yet they represent a vast transformation. Although it is unfair to blame the International Style for the sad saga of these streets, during this time its apostles held forth in the design schools, two generations of architects received little instruction about designing in these older styles and were usually not philosophically conditioned to come to the assistance of these facades.

careful facade alterations that enriched the building fronts over time, adding to their sense of self esteem. The subtle modifications of the Corley jewelry store on Richmond's bustling Broad Street illustrate this care. Even the more dramatic evolution of facade design in *Art Deco* and *Moderne* motifs that transformed the shop fronts of the same street in the 1930's and 40's sustained the visual interest of the pedestrian and often managed to relate to the building. Seen in continuously formation, they created their own new overlay of facade patterning.

Art Deco storefronts inserted into older facades create a new pattern on Richmond's Broad Street, 1935.

New buildings, usually private houses or public edifices are being constructed or proposed, which again acknowledge the power of allusion, play off historical styles, evoke particular locales and periods, or project an exaggerated sense of purpose. Indeed a traveling exhibit of facade designs is sparking the same sort of interest that attended the International Style Show in 1932. Entitled "The Presence of the Past," originally organized for the Venice Bienale of 1980, it invites a new play of ideas which has the potential of reinvigorating facade design, possibly even a decorative tradition. However most of these designs are not for commercial structures.

The allusions of Charles Moore, the stripped classicism of Michael Graves, the "decorated sheds" of Venturi and Rauch which seek to capture an "essence of place" that they liken to a Byzantine Church, are for the most part still conceived for government buildings, art museums, and private houses. Perhaps the merchants think this design too didactically related to architectural theses, and not enough to the constraints of merchandising on a street. However, shop fronts and store facades have been a more expressive vehicle for European architects, who have often used this opportunity to elucidate principles which were later realized on a larger scale.

We should hasten to add, that recovering the character of Main Street must also require resuscitating its vitality . . . and that is dependent on other actions in addition to facade design. It requires increasing the liveliness of the street through mixed use, with more residences above the store, better marketing and promotion of Main Street businesses, and ultimately some control over land use policy in the suburbs, a step that we have failed to take as a culture. Nevertheless, one need only to stroll through the downtowns rebuilt after urban renewal to fully appreciate how effectively their facades reject the eye, how seldom they activate the meanings of place that are stored in the brain.

Perhaps one of the unanticipated benefits of the renewal of downtown districts was the aggregation of enough banal structures to encourage a critical reassessment of the corporate style derived from the Modern Movement, which often characterizes this faceless development. The varied architectural offerings that are succeeding it under the loose caption of Post Modernism expand the prospect for a reconsideration of the facade.

Storefront facade renovations of the 1970's sometimes echoed in corrugated grilled or panelled packages the bland corporate behemoths derived from the Modern Movement design. This facade, now clad in vertical aluminum panels, is located on Massachusetts Avenue adjacent to I.M. Pei's Christian Science Center in Boston, Massachusetts.

Michael Graves' winning design entered in the competition for the Public Services Building in Portland, Oregon is one of the largest Post Modern facade designs. Belluschi spoke against it at a city council meeting referring to it as an "enlarged juke box or oversized beribboned Christmas package."

Venturi and Rauch's Best Products store, opposite Oxford Valley Mall, Pennsylvania, exemplifies the "decorated shed" approach of their writings and shows a recent interest in reviving a decorative tradition at an auto scale.

While some of these works represent a radical departure from the formulation of the facade—breaking down the distinction between architecture and interior design—their work often demonstrates how new technology can achieve a strong level of expressiveness for the merchant and still relate to the streetscape. It is our observation that contrary to the rhetoric about design review being a strait jacket, the quality of shop front and facade design in the historic centers of European cities where design review prevails, show that guidance has excerted a useful discipline enriching rather than inhibiting architectural work; it has encouraged an expressiveness within a framework that respects the tradition of pedestrian interest. Indeed a number of the most interesting and expensively designed store fronts are on streets that are now pedestrian malls.

Hans Hollein's dramatic shop front, in Vienna, which cracks open to reveal its riches like a geode, is a much celebrated recent example of this tradition. It is representative of the more expensive investments that owners will make when they do not feel compelled to change their image every seven to ten years; which had been the marketing trend in our own consumer society. Rising energy costs, some increase in pedestrianization, and a growing respect for the quality of facades, is beginning to affect design decisions for American storefronts. This is revealed not only by careful new designs but also by an historic preservation movement increasingly oriented to downtown business districts.

There are now 2,500 National Reg-

ister districts across the country, and in the last few years these designations have moved out of the pristine residential precincts where historic preservation got its start, into the grittier downtowns where certification of historic status now conveys tax benefits for rehabilitation. An entire literature has grown up in recent years, that describes the history of these downtown areas. This book seeks to make a contribution to that literature by capturing the dynamics of particular facades that have gone through changes in their lives—sometimes only to recover what they were. Looking at facades is

Hans Hollein's Schullin Jewelry Shop, Vienna, 1975, is in an historic district.

not yet a national pastime like other spectator sports (as it was in Renaissance Italy, when mannerist variations on classical elements would be recognized immediately by the cognoscenti). But the facade stories in this book were collected on the assumption that there is a need to look closely at how change affects a single object in the built environment. It also assumes that such an examination should be given a holistic treatment—reviewing architectural history, development context, and design intentions in the preservation, restoration, adaptive use, or commemorative regeneration of a particular facade.

Of course, some of the facades in this book are immediately interesting as works of design—cast iron classicism, Victorian, Italianate, Art Nouveau, Art Deco, even Sixties Pop. But others are intriguing because of the struggles they have gone through; some have been fought over, some have been added to or subtracted from, some have been bowdlerized and others have survived by changing their orientation. Some are contemporary acts of invention or revivalism, and others are ruins, fragments, or illusions, only as thick as a coat of paint. But, most significantly, as we examine their stories, we should be able to discern not only a range of styles and periods, but also a diversity of attitudes toward the built environment. The facades acknowledge a spectrum of concern that ranges from those who care about the facade as an artifact, similar to a house, fountain, fence, or piece of furniture, and therefore seek to preserve it even if this means totally removing the facade from its context in the environment, to those who see an old facade as something that can be removed if a new one can be better designed to fill its place—with perhaps a token left behind—a mural or a salvaged object.

These contrasting positions are in fact contiguous as they come full circle—resulting in the same condition—the removal of a facade from its context in the cityscape—though they reach that conclusion by different routes. In the first case, a facade is treated as an artifact and removed for its preservation, and in the other case, a facade is replaced because something is considered better or more useful. In the book these two positions are illustrated in the story of the Art Noveau facade of the Gnomen Copy which was to have been removed to the Boston Museum of Fine Art and in the tale of the surviving Walrus fragments salvaged from the Alaska Commercial Building facade and applied to the new bank tower which took its place. The long curve that connects these two positions is marked with the facade stories we present herein.

We have tried to make this book a representative sampling of attitudes toward this one element in the built environment, but we by no means endorse all of the solutions which we have uncovered! Our own position is conservative; we are generally in favor of keeping older facades, partially out of the conviction that the older streetscapes hold more interest and more memories, and partially in the dour belief that they are not likely to be re-

placed with anything of comparable architectural quality. We are skeptical of the salvage jobs and bowdlerizations which have been the price of survival for some of the facades profiled here. But we would probably keep the facade shells as armatures supporting place meaning in a built environment which has suffered as much future shock as any other part of our culture. We have been mildly satiric about the polyester suiting of Main Street and kits of kitsch in Olde English, da-glo, mini-mansard ad nauseum. We are disturbed that some readers of Robert Venturi's *Learning from Las Vegas* come away from the experience tolerating the corporate visual ripoff of Main Street by out-of-town sign salesmen. To acknowledge this phenomenon should not sustain a false determinism that "main street is almost alright." Celebrating the special aesthetic of the Las Vegas strip or Sunset Boulevard should not provide an academic apology for imposing big signs and flashing lights on Main Streets everywhere.

When looking at Main Streetscape, we tend to balance the values of continuity and conformity—tilting toward the latter when a streetscape has a well defined and respected character of architectural elements—a particular historical imagery, or a citizenry attuned to its qualities. We believe that individual storefronts should serve in the chorus, and be only as flamboyant as the other choral robes. It is our intention, however, to provide enough information in the following pages, that these issues can be debated, and to that end,

we present the context—both the physical situation on the streetscape, and the particular socio-economic milieu that affected the design decisions.

Facade Stories is principally concerned with the care and treatment of old faces; we readily acknowledge the need for a companion volume which would examine some of the new storefronts. We are modestly optimistic that there will be a renaissance of efforts under the aegis of what is being called the Post Modern Movement. We trust it can match in quality the Art Deco design done on Main Street during the depression, when it was the only source of income for some architects. A recent neighborhood business district rehabilitation in Buffalo with its modern *moderne* theme, indicates a return to that sensibility, and appears to be one of the most comprehensive storefront renovation projects in the country.

In the meantime, we hope that this book can achieve its mission—encouraging a broader constituency of Americans to pay increasing attention to the faces of older commercial buildings. We trust that through an examination of these different case studies, people can become involved in the conservation and preservation of older facades.

Alas, precious little has been written about storefronts by the handful of American architectural critics. Their energies are usually not focused on Main Street, but on major new architectural projects. Perhaps it is fitting then to close this introduction with the words of an architectural critic who recognizes the importance of Main Street faces. Writing about the Gnomon Copy story—the saving in place rather than the salvaging for museum display of the only Art Nouveau storefront in Cambridge—Ada Louise Huxtable's article for the *New York Times* included this statement:

"Commercial architecture at its best is a pragmatically and magnificently American achievement. Scholars have placed it in the mainstream of art history . . . As these buildings are lost through thoughtless demolition or remodeling, the sterile void they leave in the urban environment has become tragically evident. Their sense of place, style, and the American past are irreplaceable . . . a shopfront, a small factory, part of a town—these are not really such small things."

It is our intention in the following chapters to demonstrate that the store-

Walrus fragment from Alaska Commercial facade now affixed to a wall of California First Bank, which replaces it. This bank is owned by a Japanese corporation and takes its design inspiration from Japanese fortresses. Perhaps the walruses can be viewed as a Shinto offering to this building's antecedent.

18

Architect Peter Nowak and other designers are using styles from the 1920's, 30's, and 40's to renovate the facades of some thirty buildings in Buffalo's Broadway-Fillmore neighborhood business district. Underwritten by community development block grants matched by private investment, the intent is to create a special look on buildings that had no particular facade character before the renovations.

fronts of Main Street are indeed "not such small things." But we affirm that this significance not only relates to the physical fabric of our cities and towns, but also to the mental landscape that citizens carry around with them in their heads. Facades are more deeply etched in the mind because they combine the two connotations which we mentioned at the beginning of this chapter. As special treatments for the fronts of buildings they are memorable for composition or for the particular effect of a decorative pattern or sometimes for their combined impact as components of a larger streetscape stage. And their deception of "false fronts" distrusted by designers of the International Style is transcended by a larger reality—the artifice whether grandiose or trivial, whether cast iron palace or brass pipe door handle, intrigues with its claims for our attention—with its capacity to elicit associations. Will another generation struggle to save the bland and constricted fronts of most contemporary commercial structures? It seems very unlikely that they will evoke similar tales of ingenuity and persistence which often helped to save or restore the facades we reveal herein. Disfigured or even obliterated, the associations with these facades remained in the mind, and compelled some redemptive actions—even token salvage.

Perhaps then, this book will be useful not only to those who wish to survey a variety of approaches toward the conservation of old facades but also to those who are interested in designing new facades that can sustain a sense of place. The facades in this book have

managed to do that, and their survival or regeneration, albeit sometimes in a fragmented state, bears witness to the concern of the people who made that emotive connection with them. We hope that out of these many tales of older facades will come some clear perception of how these emotive ties can

be evoked in new ones. For ultimately, it is this bonding to place which supports an ethic for the conservation of the built environment. We trust it can help those engaged in contemporary professional practice to value and then more effectively realize that ethic in their own work.

Art Nouveau facade. Gnomon Copy, Cambridge, Massachusetts.

1 · Facade Survivors: *Originals still in Service*

No matter how comprehensive the demolition of urban renewal, no matter how persuasive the aluminum clapboard salesmen, and no matter how determined the landlord to accommodate a new use, there are usually facade survivors who have managed to endure because of their architectural character or historic interest. They inspire a certain affection which encourages a feeling of proprietorship. Typically, the facade survivors in this chapter had someone to look after them. Leavitt and Peirce's distinguished facade survived through a succession of responsible owners and the benevolent interest of nearby Harvard University. Jessop's facade, a gem in a streetscape of eyesores, has survived and expanded through the protection of owners interested in upholding the firm's classic image. While both these owners sought prestige because of the nature of their business— Leavitt and Peirce as a tobacco shop catering to an exclusive clientele, Jessop's as a jewelry store—our other two facade survivors changed to corporate businesses and remained intact only through the concern of local citizens. Gnomon Copy's unique Art Nouveau facade was saved by the concerted action of several parties, including an art professor, the local historic commission, and Boston's Museum of Fine Arts, who convinced the photocopy franchise to keep and maintain such an asset. And McDonald's agreed to respect the character of the restrained townhouse facade on Walnut Street in Philadelphia under pressure from an active merchants' group determined to maintain the neighborhood's identity.

Facades are image-makers, so it is not surprising that those facades best cared for are the ones catering to an image-conscious clientele. As a facade leaves its imprint on a place over time, the public begins to feel it belongs to them. Consequently, poems have been written about the decorative carved Indian in Leavitt and Peirce's doorway; and Jessop's ornate street clock, originally installed as an attention-getter, has become a public fixture for checking one's watch or waiting for an engagement. Decorative elements can help in this way to insure a more devoted clientele.

Without a proprietor concerned about appearance, however, the public must become involved to conserve a streetscape. Often, determined individuals have had to step in to save a facade, but in the past ten years merchants' associations, preservation groups, and other civic-minded organizations have increasingly performed this role. These stories show that even the best facades need the tenacity and vigilance of the caring few.

An Aromatic Tradition Sustains a Facade

Leavitt and Peirce   Cambridge, Massachusetts

Across the street from Harvard Yard, the dignified facade of Leavitt and Peirce has changed little since the store opened nearly a century ago. A succession of sensitive owners and a close relationship with Harvard University have enabled this facade to remain intact.

In 1885, a four-bay extension to an existing commercial building provided new storefront space in Harvard Square. The first two stories were soon occupied by the firm of Leavitt and Peirce. On the ground floor, owners Fred H. Leavitt and Wallace W. Peirce sold pipes, tobacco, cigars and other smoking-related articles. The second floor housed a billiard (and pool table) room.

Leavitt and Peirce quickly became established as both a high-quality to-bacco seller and as, in the words of the *Harvard Crimson,* the "unofficial headquarters for Harvard men." Its windows were well-known as the display area for announcements to athletes and members of Harvard clubs, and the store served as the branch ticket agency of the Harvard Athletic Association. Messrs. Leavitt and Peirce befriended many undergraduates and were in turn made honorary members of a number of Harvard clubs and associations. Several prominent graduates of Harvard patronized Leavitt and Peirce while still students; Samuel Eliot Morison was there introduced to "fearful and wonderful brands of cigarettes," while Walter Muir Whitehill bought his first pipe at its counter.

When the founders of Leavitt and Peirce both died in the early 1920's, the store was acquired by Frank Knapp and Fred Moore. They had been encouraged to purchase the establishment by Harvard's president, Abbott Lawrence Lowell, as well as by other members of the University community, who, the *Crimson* reported, "were eager to have the ownership pass to others whose interests are likewise the interests of Harvard. . . ." The new owners made no major changes and Leavitt and Peirce continued to be a popular shop and meeting place.

By the late 1940's, though, the business was floundering. Fred Moore's daughter had by this time acquired the store and she attempted to diversify it by installing a hamburger counter. Business was still poor, and Moore was ready to liquidate before her money ran out entirely. Once again, members of Harvard intervened. Loath to see the store die, David McCord, poet and litterateur, approached tobacconists—and Harvard graduates—Richard and William Erlich of the David P. Erlich Company in Boston. Could the Erlichs buy

Left: The 1300–1316 block of Massachusetts Avenue as it appeared in 1913. Right: Though all around it has changed, the Leavitt and Peirce facade remains the same today, with its gilt lettering and decorative trim. The carved figure over the door proffering cigars, supposed to be an Indian, looks more like an opera singer.

Leavitt and Peirce and save this Harvard tradition?

Indeed they could; the Erlichs bought Leavitt and Peirce in 1956. They retained the store's original name and facade and sought to restore the interior to its previous club-like appearance. The Erlichs removed the hamburger counter and covered the walls with old Harvard Varsity photographs, footballs and crew oars from Harvard victories, and tobacco memorabilia. Replicas of the old-fashioned cigar store counters were put into place, and the store once again became a living Harvard tradition. In fact, the Erlichs were so enamored of the shop's legacy that they published a book of essays and poems by well-known Harvard graduates entitled 75 *Aromatic Years of Leavitt and Peirce in Recollection of 31 Harvard Men.* When the Erlichs retired in 1979, they turned down several offers from large conglomerate organizations and sold the company instead to a group headed by their general manager, Paul J. MacDonald. They had feared that a corporate owner would make drastic changes, and they chose MacDonald to ensure that, in the words of William P. Erlich, "the quality tradition be retained."

The Leavitt and Peirce facade maintains a feeling of the nineteenth century; as William P. Erlich aptly noted, "Enough dust is left on so that it is not a 'modern' building." The discreet gold-on-black sign and stencilled windows, subdued paint, and attractive window displays all contribute to this feeling.

Decorative elements give the facade a special appeal. The door handle is in the shape of a whimsically oversized pipe, while above the door a carved wooden Indian maiden proffers cigars. The use of the Indian as a smoke shop trade symbol originated in seventeenth-century England, when the English first imported tobacco from the Colonies and associated it with the natives from the New World. Americans later adopted the symbolic Indian figure, turning out scores of them during the latter half of the nineteenth century as redundant wooden shipbuilders sought new employment. The carvers often interpreted Indian characteristics very loosely; the Leavitt and Peirce maiden's features and body more closely resemble those of an opera singer than of a native American. Representational trade signs served to identify businesses to a largely illiterate clientele and to make the location of a shop memorable before the institution of street numbers. The Leavitt and Peirce maiden was found by McCord in Littleton, Massachusetts in the 1950's; her function has always been primarily decorative.

CONTEXT

Leavitt and Peirce is one of the few businesses retaining an air of stability amongst the ephemeral stores of Harvard Square. The shop has kept pace by careful diversification, offering a variety of men's luxury accessories as well as highly-crafted games such as chess and backgammon. An alcove of the shop has been leased to a small antique business, and the second floor is no longer used. Leavitt and Peirce appeals to a specialized but devoted clientele of tobacco connoisseurs from Cambridge and around the world—and, of course, to Harvard students, whose athletic notices are still posted in the store's windows. Leavitt and Peirce does not try to call attention to itself, but its contribution to the community is nonetheless appreciated. As David McCord wrote about the Erlichs and Leavitt and Peirce in 75 *Aromatic Years,* the proprietors have brought back to at least one foot of Harvard Square the universal dignity of an old tavern sign aswing among the screaming headlines of Main Street, U.S.A.

The door handle is a pipe.

21

Jessop's in 1936. Even then it was a dignified holdout against the surrounding decay.

Elegant Street Clock Keeps an Old Facade in Fashion

Jessop's Jewelry Store   San Diego, California

The 1907 Jessop's clock, with its twenty dials and native California jewels, stands in the downtown business district of San Diego. It is an elegant clock, a testament to a past era of commercial refinement. And this treasure has created and sustained another landmark: the elegant 1898 facade of Jessop's Jewelry Store, which has maintained its original appearance throughout its seventy-five-year life.

The handmade clock was designed by the store owner and jeweler, Joseph Jessop, in 1907. It is twenty-one feet high and has twenty dials, twelve of which tell the time of all the nations as well as the second, minute, hour, date and month. Embellished with native stones of jade, agate, tourmaline and topaz, the clock won a gold medal at the Sacramento State Fair in 1907 and has been a San Diego landmark ever since.

When the Jessop family moved its jewelry store to this downtown site in 1927, they took their prized clock with them. Jessop's new home was an 1898 brick building that had originally served as a fire house. Some years earlier the building had been converted into offices, with two retail shops on the bot-

The facade today. Jessop's has expanded into the neighboring building, and facade detailing has been carefully replicated. The grey coloring adds dignity to the structure, and the shop floor awning is correctly proportioned. The Victorian street lamp has disappeared.

Checking one's watch. Street clocks have served this public function for centuries.

tom floor. Jessop's moved in to one side of the building, placed its clock outside, and started renovations on its half of the facade. Eighty thousand dollars later, the Jessop's facade was an attractive compliment to its clock. The new marble storefront was embellished with a walnut clerestory with bronze, onyx and gold leaf detailing.

The Jessop's Jewelry Store has remained in the Jessop family since its opening day in 1907, and the store has been in its present location since 1927. The facade has undergone few changes since the initial renovation. In 1950, the two stores that shared the Jessop's building sold their space to the jeweler, and the Jessops continued their original facade design to the other half of the building. At this time, the entire facade was repainted to charcoal gray, creating a quiet understated backdrop to the extravagantly ornamented clock.

CONTEXT

Jessop's Jewelry Store is an intricately detailed landmark in an otherwise banal streetscape. San Diego's Fifth Avenue, which extends between the historic gaslight district and the business district, is glutted with the box-like buildings of the 1960s and older facades that have been unsympathetically modernized with blank panels. The distinctive Jessop's facade, anchored by a landmark clock and preserved by a caring family, is a lone example of commercial quality—waiting, perhaps, for surrounding merchants to return to their senses.

Museum Offer Moves Photocopy Franchise To Keep One-of-a-Kind Facade

Gnomon Copy   Cambridge, Massachusetts

This Art Nouveau facade, with its sweeping curves and floral detailing, could be considered a work of art, even a museum piece. In fact, the Boston Museum of Fine Arts deemed it precisely that, and this acknowledgement of the facade's significance helped to save it from demolition.

The block of brick buildings that stretches from 1300 to 1316 Massachusetts Avenue, though apparently uniform, is actually comprised of several distinct buildings representing different periods and styles. At the corner of Massachusetts Avenue and Linden Street, a four-story, seven-bay structure was erected by a merchant named Dolton in 1869. This dignified building, with a mansard roof and pedimented window heads, was in the Second Empire style, and although buildings of this size and style had been popular in Boston for about ten years, it was considered advanced for Cambridge. Its use was appropriate to its location: while the ground floor was devoted to retail stores, the upper levels served as dormitories for nearby Harvard University.

In 1900, the mansard roof was removed, and the building was heightened two stories and combined with its adjacent neighbors to form a still larger commercial/dormitory complex called the Fairfax. A central doorway was installed at the inside corner of the old Dolton building, providing a link between the two previously unrelated structures and identifying the block with the Fairfax name.

A new facade was erected next to the Fairfax doorway at 1304 Massachusetts Avenue in 1904. Providing an attractive contrast to the heavy masonry of the doorway, this new storefront was of wood and glass and in the manner of Art Nouveau, an artistic style popular in the graphic and decorative arts but unusual in architecture.

The architects responsible for the facade, J.R. Coolidge and H.J. Carlson, were known for several Cambridge buildings that were formal, conservative, and of a much larger scale than this storefront. It is not clear why they turned to Art Nouveau here, but John Coolidge, Professor of Fine Arts at Harvard University and the architect's nephew, suggests that it might have been his uncle's growing interest in other fields of art, a pursuit that eventually led to his becoming the director of the Boston Museum of Fine Arts. The one-story facade boasts the curvilinear, sinuous lines characteristic of Art Nouveau and a typically asymmetrical doorway. The brass door handle is long and slender, and the leaf-like fronds at its top and bottom are derived from those popular in graphic design of the period.

The facade was installed for a retail shoe store, and was later occupied by a combination newsstand and shoe repair business known as Felix's. This business did no real damage to the facade, but obscured it with a large metal awning and a newsstand that extended across the front of the shop. The owner was also lax about maintaining the varnished wood. When Felix's vacated the store in 1970, Gnomon Copy, a fran-

The 1300–1316 block of Massachusetts Avenue in 1913. Coes and Young, Co. facade, at left of photo, is now Gnomon Copy.

Felix's Shoe Shine in 1968: Art Nouveau and Nixon.

The sculpted irregularity of Art Nouveau still functions well as an entryway, though a copy center ignores the potential of the glass expanse. The "Gnomon Copy" name is reflected off the large purple sign, unseen above the photograph.

chise of photocopy businesses, moved in. Gnomon Copy removed the metal awning, revealing the underlying facade and also announced their plans to replace this decorative storefront with something more "modern."

Opposition mounted quickly, led by the Cambridge Historical Commission and John Coolidge. While the Commission documented the history and significance of the facade, Coolidge and a local architect, Heyward Cutting, approached the Museum of Fine Arts with an unusual acquisition recommendation: the Art Nouveau storefront, an early work of one of the Museum's former directors. The curators agreed to accept the facade if it were otherwise to be demolished.

Coolidge then arranged a meeting with the head of Harvard Realty Trust, owner of the building, while Lawrence McKinney, another local enthusiast, met with the owner of Gnomon Copy. Armed with the documentation of the facade's significance and a statement of interest from the Museum, they convinced the owner and tenant that the facade was worth preserving. Gnomon

Lacy, intertwined forms grace even the door handle and keyhole.

Copy agreed to leave the museum piece right where it was, and Harvard Realty Trust agreed to complete any necessary restoration work.

Refurbishing of the facade was minimal. All that was required was a sanding and varnishing of the wood members, and Gnomon Copy has agreed to be responsible for revarnishing the wood every two years. The project received some good publicity when Ada Louise Huxtable featured it in a 1971 *The New York Times* article on preserving small-scale commercial buildings. The refinished storefront is indeed "rare and charming," as she notes, although the standard corporate Gnomon sign is certainly not. The sign meets city ordinance requirements but nevertheless looms over the facade in an overwhelming manner. A smaller sign, of some material other than illuminated purple plastic, would be a considerable improvement.

CONTEXT

The offer by the Museum of Fine Arts to acquire this facade raised questions of where to preserve: in the safety of a museum or in the context of the street. The approach of an earlier generation of architectural afficionados, men like Henry Francis Dupont of Winterthur Museum and Electra Havemeyer Webb of Shelburn Village, was to amass elements and fragments of buildings from around the country and establish them in a new museum setting. More recently, preservationists have argued that the context is a large part of a building's meaning, and that saving a room or a facade in an isolated setting is not really saving it at all. Ada Louise Huxtable concurs: "one good storefront on a city street is worth a dozen in the Smithsonian or the Boston Fine Arts."

In the case of Gnomon Copy, sending the facade to the Boston Museum would have been unquestionably better than demolishing it. Retaining it on the street, though, where it continues to add variety and where passers-by can see it daily, is an even better solution. All that is missing is an interpretive plaque or sign, so that viewers could understand the facade's significance and better appreciate its presence on Massachusetts Avenue.

After restoration: Still a graceful resident in a coherent streetscape. Graphics are subdued for McDonald's and do not overwhelm; recessed dark glass cuts down glare of modern interior.

1706 Walnut St. before restoration.

Street Association Challenges
A Fast-Food Giant And Saves A Facade

McDonald's   Walnut Street, Philadelphia, Pennsylvania

If the owner does not take responsibility for preserving a notable facade, often the community must step into this role. Fast-food chains are notorious for intrusive, unappealing facades which disrupt the streetscape. The merchants of the Walnut Street Association of Philadelphia, however, organized quickly and effectively upon hearing that the McDonald's Corporation planned to open a restaurant in their fashionable shopping district. They succeeded in maintaining a facade that supports the quality of their street and pleases the new owner.

The three-story limestone structure at 1706 Walnut Street was built in the late nineteenth century as a private residence. By about 1920 this neighborhood was no longer exclusively residential, and a display window was added to the ground floor in order to accommodate retail use. A series of businesses have occupied the building since that time, but in spite of frequent changes in ownership few renovations were ever made to the attractive Italianate facade. In 1976, a fire destroyed the interior; the building was boarded up and unoccupied until it was purchased by the McDonald's Corporation.

One merchant who was particularly interested in the fate of this location was Ruth Ferber, manager of the adjacent Jacques Ferber Furs and also president of the Walnut Street Association. Mrs. Ferber did not favor a food franchise next to her fur salon but, since zoning regulations permit restaurants on Walnut Street, she knew there was little chance of blocking McDonald's occupation of the building. She and other members of the Walnut Street Association were, however, determined to fight the installation of McDonald's standard packaged facade and signage.

McDonald's executives learned that the Walnut Street Association was concerned about their project and visited Mrs. Ferber at her shop. She expressed concern about a garish storefront and requested that McDonald's design a facade with "dignity" that was "in keeping with the quality shops on our street." They produced photographs of McDonald's in other American cities where existing facades had been sensitively renovated, and the Walnut Street Association hoped that such a project could be carried out in their neighborhood.

The details were resolved in a series of City Hall meetings between company representatives and Walnut Street property owners, followed by a lively and well-attended zoning hearing. The McDonald's executives believed the location was a desirable one and, perhaps because they had met with organized community opposition elsewhere, were willing to compromise in order to reach an agreement. The outcome was a decision to retain the existing facade, and the Philadelphia Art Commission was to have approval over any signs.

The architect for the project, George E. Murray of Gilder, Murray and Associates, made as few alterations to the facade as possible. He stripped layers of paint off the limestone, cleaned the facade with steel brushes, and recast the damaged plaster corbels and lintels. The entire front was painted an antique white color to blend with adjoining buildings. The restaurant required a fairly large entranceway, but in order to avoid violating the integrity of the facade Murray designed a recessed inner entrance of smoked glass where the earlier display window had been. This solution creates a shallow arcade, and the McDonald's typographic and logotype signs are suspended in the existing window and entrance fenestrations at a height that matches the clerestory windows of Jacques Ferber Furs next door. Although the typography is contemporary and does utilize the McDonald's arches, the signs themselves are small and are in suitable shades of light and dark bronze.

Ruth Ferber is pleased with the results. Although she had feared that McDonald's would be an unwelcome and conspicuous presence, she says that one is not even aware that the building is a restaurant until directly in front of it. This McDonald's is notable precisely for this *lack* of distinguishing features.

CONTEXT

McDonald's was only one of the first in a series of fast food restaurants that have opened on Walnut Street during the past few years. Though near historic Rittenhouse Square, this area is not protected by historic district status and, unfortunately, the later arrivals have not cooperated so thoroughly with the requests of the Walnut Street Association, whose legal control is limited. Litter and noise have increased on this previously dignified street.

In an effort to maintain the quality of Walnut Street and its surroundings, the City Planning Commission has recently proposed an ordinance requiring clean-ups, design and color control over facades, and limits on the number of franchise restaurants on any one Philadelphia street. While this comprehensive ordinance may meet with too much business opposition to pass, it is likely that the Walnut Street Association will be assisted by some type of statutory protection in the future.

II · **Facades Restored:** *Discovering the Past*

The pleasure of this chapter is in viewing the "after" pictures which peel back the accretions on some facades and recover their prior identity. While there is an old saying that the eye is blind to what the mind cannot see, these pictures make it clear to many what sometimes only a discerning few could see before. Ecker Drug in Corning, New York, is a particular favorite in this regard, because it was hard to imagine, if one had not lived in Corning before, what existed behind the glass slip cover that wrapped the facade in the sixties.

These really are stories of the time in American life when Main Street was beset by the twin pandoras of urban renewal demolition and facade packaging to compete with the corporate look of the shopping malls. In two of the stories, old facades emerge triumphant amidst the rubble of downtown renewal. In Winooski the old facade visually dominates the downtown, the sight lines unfortunately enlarged by the clearance; it has served as the catalyst for a broader program of rejuvenation which included design improvements on the remaining business buildings and the rehabilitation of two large mills. In Detroit, the restoration of Cornice and Slate was undertaken privately, and it has not had the same effect on the surrounding area.

The Galveston and New Harmony projects illustrate the importance of having a third party, the public interest non-profit organization, which can often develop a more innovative approach than government, and take risks for a public purpose that private investors would not initially undertake. H. M. Trueheart was the first building to be renovated in Galveston's historic Strand district demonstrating the clairvoyance of the Junior League, later backed up by a series of projects now that Historic Galveston Inc. is operating. New

Harmony still has a utopian glow due to the beneficence of its well financed non-profit organization. Obviously not every town has the kind of historic associations or architectural patrimony that will attract some outside philanthropic investments, but many do have community funds often used for basic social needs, which could make investments in preservation projects as a part of their business portfolio.

Several of the stories give fairly comprehensive accounts of the details of restoration which sometimes required extensive research about original elements and suitable replacement materials. The Ecker Drug facade, for example, lost its cornice and much of its column ornamentation during the installation of pyroceram panels, and these had to be carefully reconstructed. However, in Traverse City, Michigan, it was deemed too expensive to reconstruct the rooftop pediment. In each case, designers undertook research which should interest the more technically inclined reader, and more of this material is included in the appendix.

It is worth noting that a "loveable object," a wildlife ornament, was an important part of the drama of three restoration stories. The replacement or refurbishment of eagles, difficult to achieve at a time when craftsmen are no longer part of the building process, occupied the attention of the restorers. The architect for the Detroit Cornice and Slate found "one of the last craftsmen left in the world" in a downtown body shop to carry out the repair and reworking of the building's pressed metal facade and to supervise the recovery of a metal eagle. Eagles for Portsmouth's Emporium and the Winooski Block were handcrafted again in wood, adding a dimension of public interest and attendant publicity as dormant skills were revived.

Junior League Reveals a Colorful Facade And Helps Bring a Street Back to Life

H. M. Trueheart & Co.   Galveston, Texas

The Strand, Galveston's historic commercial district, was such a major financial center toward the end of the nineteenth century that it was known as the "Wall Street of the Southwest." Yet by the 1960's its grandeur had faded; the Strand was little more than a few rows of deteriorating cast iron and brick facades threatened by demolition

for parking lots to accommodate the business district, which had shifted a few blocks further from the waterfront. It took a women's civic organization, the Galveston Junior League, to see that behind the peeling paint, there were magnificent structures. They were the first to take one, the former H. M. Trueheart & Co. building, and refur-

bish the facade, pointing the way toward a major commercial revitalization project, which is making the Strand once more a center of activity.

The story of this facade begins with a businessman, John O. Trueheart, who established a land agent business in Galveston in 1857. His son, Henry M. Trueheart, entered the business following the Civil War, and the firm took the name of H. M. Trueheart & Co., expanding to include real estate and general tax agents and stock brokers. In 1881, the firm commissioned the Irish-born architect Nicholas J. Clayton, whose work was already well-known in Galveston, to design a new fireproof office building.

The polychromatic facade of the resulting building was an elaborate combination of a variety of materials and architectural elements. A contemporary description cites "red brick, with panels, mouldings, chamfers, string courses, etc., of black and white bricks and carved freestone, in relief," not to mention the French casement doorways and the "three light iron columns, tastefully cast, and finished in green and bronze." Clayton based his design upon the fashionable Italian Renaissance revival style, but it was the detailing and color that made the facade exceptional. The architect used both pressed brick of several moulds and patterns and carved stone to create the polychromatic effect in the upper stories. As originally designed, the ground floor facade was an arcade of casement doors, also ornamented.

H. M. Trueheart & Co. moved into the first floor in January of 1882, and they leased the second floor to two attorneys. The firm of H. M. Trueheart changed its name to that of a later partner but continued at the same address, and it enjoyed a reputation not only as the state's oldest real estate firm but also one of the largest. The building was continuously occupied by the second-floor attorneys until they retired in the 1950's and by a realty agency until 1958.

After restoration in 1980: meticulous craftsmanship brings an exuberant facade back to life.

View of the Trueheart building at the turn of the century.

By the 1950's, however, Galveston's downtown focus had changed. The Strand was no longer a commercial focal point, and the Trueheart building, like many others, became vacant. In the mid-1960's the City proposed to raze the area as part of an urban renewal project, but the community was not ready to see the district disappear. A local referendum defeated the proposal, and shortly thereafter, in 1969, the Galveston Junior League decided to take the first step toward renovating the area. It purchased the dilapidated Trueheart building and began investigating how best to rejuvenate the tarnished facade. The League's interest in renovating the building was threefold: 1) to revive the former integrity of the building itself, 2) to demonstrate the contribution that the renewal of the Strand could make to the future of Galveston, and 3) to provide the League with a handsome building for its headquarters.

The ground floor arcade had been closed off in the middle, but the facade was otherwise unaltered structurally. The League discovered that much of the polychrome brickwork had been painted, and the problem was to discover a method of paint removal that would not damage the slip-glazed brick. Sandblasting, waterblasting, and a process that involved the use of walnut or pecan hulls were all rejected, and finally a NASA painter proposed a chemical process that proved successful. After reviewing a number of bids and discussing the project with contractors

Wooden trim shows Clayton's high-spirited, free interpretation of decorative elements.

and architect Charles Zwiener, the League approved a budget of about $35,000 to renovate the building inside and out.

During this renovation, completed in 1970, the contractor removed the paint from the bricks, painted the wooden trim and pediment, and stripped the entry doors to their natural wood. In 1979, a $20,000 federal matching grant administered by the Texas Historical Commission funded a second restoration that finally returned the building to its original appearance, with the exception of the arcade. Taft Architects of Houston analyzed and supervised work on the facade, including pointing of the brick and repainting of the cut limestone. In the spring of 1979, Galveston County officials and Rita Clements, the wife of Governor Bill Clements, joined in the celebration to dedicate the build-

ing and to herald the work of the Junior League, one of the first groups in Texas to restore a commercial building.

CONTEXT

Established in 1838, the City of Galveston served by the middle of that century as the point of entry for most goods shipped to inland Texas. Following the Civil War the area of the city that bordered the wharves, the Strand, gained in importance as banking, wholesale, commission, manufacturing and shipping interests thrived.

The commercial buildings which housed these businesses have a particular identity. Like the Trueheart building, many were the work of the city's most prominent architect, Nicholas Clayton, whose versatile use of revival styles create an architectural unity which has survived partially because of

neglect. For, despite the opening of a Grand Opera House in 1895 which marked the city's role as the regional cultural center, Galveston soon went into decline. Devastated by a great hurricane which killed more than 6,000 residents in 1900, the city was in the long term unable to compete with Houston after the opening of the Houston ship channel. Galveston's economy has revived only in the past decade as the port area expanded, posing a new threat to the old commercial architecture, of which the Trueheart building, though on a small scale, is perhaps the most flamboyant example.

"The Strand is alive and well today because of the pioneering work of the Galveston Junior League," declared Peter Brink, Executive Director of the Galveston Historical Foundation. Soon after the League's restoration of the Trueheart Building and the adjacent First National Bank, the GHF, with a grant from the Moody Foundation, started a $215,000 revolving fund to buy and restore the commercial buildings of the Strand. By 1980, with 20 buildings rehabilitated, 5 restaurants, 17 shops, 32 apartments and 35,000 square feet of offices have been created, with more than $6,000,000 in investment committed. The H. M. Trueheart & Co. building, which today houses the office and catering project of the Junior League, visibly reveals the success of this pioneering program.

A Facade Keeps Faith With Main Street Scale And Expands Behind It

The Owen Block and J. Breith Building   New Harmony, Indiana

The Owen Block and adjacent J. Breith building demonstrate that, just as you can't judge a book by its cover, you can't always determine a building's interior configuration from its facade. Two apparently unrelated facades have been connected inside, a solution that is not new but that should be employed more often to save Main Street buildings. This assemblage demonstrates how one can successfully create a substantial interior space while still retaining a small-scale, varied streetfront.

Increasing prosperity toward the end of the nineteenth century in New Harmony produced several new buildings in the town's commercial district. The Owen Block, a group of structures with exuberant facades, was built in 1882 by the grandsons of the town patriarch Robert Owen. The Block occupied a corner lot and originally was comprised of two identical three-story facade on Main Street and a similar two-story facade on Church Street, both of cast iron below and pressed metal above.

The cornices were handsomely detailed with moldings that depict the rays of the sun.

The Owen Block buildings were connected and were used at first for an agricultural supply business. Later owners partitioned the inside space to create separate stores, and the buildings served a variety of commercial retail uses. In 1921, the Main Street corner facade was demolished to make room for a bank building, which remains today. The town of New Harmony slumbered during the 1950's, and many of the commercial buildings fell into disrepair. It was not until the 1970's that they received a new lease on life, when the commercial district became one facet of a major rehabilitation project. The work was conducted by a newly-formed group, Historic New Harmony Inc., whose founder and president is Ralph Grayson Schwarz.

The Owen Block as it originally appeared, with a two-section facade. Right section remains today; left section was torn down and replaced by bank building in 1921.

The Owen Block today, after careful restoration of the cast iron and pressed metal facade. Note the simple yet elegant lines of the brackets and decoration.

Schwarz, experienced in the preservation field as founder of the National Historic Preservation Fund, developed a thorough restoration plan for New Harmony's commercial buildings. In accordance with his belief that "simply cleaning and repainting a facade is an easy task . . . true restoration is another matter entirely," Schwarz assembled and directed a coterie of researchers, consultants, and workmen. In the case of the Owen Block, workers spent months scraping paint from the Main Street facade of wood and plaster in order to find the original color. Missing pieces of the facade, such as the ground-floor corner pilasters, were researched through photographic archives and carefully recreated. The Church Street facade had long since lost its 1880's storefront, and Schwarz cleared away the existing badly fenestrated brick surface. He restored the original corner pilasters to match the Main Street facade, and replaced the storefront with new mullioned glass modeled after the facade as it appeared in early photographs. The results live up to the Historic New Harmony, Inc.

restoration maxim that "anything worth doing is worth doing well."

Historic New Harmony provided the financing, acquired from philanthropic funds, for the exterior research and restoration. The interior restorations and the commercial endeavors therein were financed with risk capital. The Church Street facade now contains the Soup to Nuts gift shop and The Greenroom restaurant. The Main Street interior plan is, however, more intriguing.

Schwarz was confronted with a common problem: how to house a large establishment on a Main Street consisting only of small stores. Unlike many before him, he decided neither to tear down existing structures nor to add on vertically. Instead, he expanded horizontally—but only inside. The facades were left untouched, while the interiors of the Main Street Owen Block facade and the adjacent 1893 J. Breith building were joined to become a single, sweeping space. Project architect Robert Hatch reported that this solution posed no major structural problems. This large interior now comfort-

ably houses the New Harmony Gallery of Contemporary Art, a group affiliated with Historic New Harmony, Inc., whose gallery provides a showplace for the work of regional artists and craftsmen. The complex is a successful testimony to the increasingly creative approach of preservationists.

CONTEXT

New Harmony had good reason to embark on a large-scale rehabilitation program, for its history is colorful and worthy of attention. The town was founded in 1814 by the Harmony Society, a group of Lutheran separatists from Germany. Led by George Rapp, the Harmonists chose 30,000 acres on the Wabash River as the site for their religious, economically communal settlement. After a prosperous ten years, the group sold its town to another hopeful utopian, Robert Owen. The group led by Owen survived for only two years, but many of the scientists and educators who remained kept the community alive. Various New Harmony residents went on to make major contributions to American science, education, and women's suffrage, as well as the founding of the Smithsonian Institute.

New Harmony had bursts of prosperity during the next century, but by the 1960's it had become run down, attracting little attention save that of one woman, Jane Blaffer Owen. Mrs. Owen was the wife of Kenneth Dale Owen, a descendant of the town's earlier leader, and successful oil geologist. She is the daughter of a founder of Humble Oil (now Exxon). She began to direct her resources into New Harmony, and soon interested a board member of the Blaffer Trust, Ralph Grayson Schwarz. Mr. Schwarz, whom Mrs. Owen brought to New Harmony for limited project work, independently fell in love with the town and sought to initiate a large-scale redevelopment project. In 1973, the Indiana State Legislature established a New Harmony Commission to investigate legislation, funding and the possibility of a development corporation, and the following year the Commission created Historic New Harmony, Inc., to carry out a comprehensive restoration plan.

Today New Harmony boasts a myriad of restored buildings as well as contemporary architecture including the Roofless Church designed by Philip

Interior of the art gallery, looking back towards the facades of the Breith Building, on the left, and the Owen Block, on the right. A successful fusion of space behind two distinct facades.

Johnson and the Atheneum by Richard Meier. Historic New Harmony, Inc., maintains exhibits and conducts tours of the new architecture as well as of its historic properties. The State of Indiana has completed Interstate Highway 64, providing improved tourism access to the town, and has developed a nearby 3,200-acre recreation area. The total cost of the New Harmony development has been close to $21 million, and, in

comparison, the Owen Block seems rather insignificant. But, as Ralph Grayson Schwarz has observed, the message of New Harmony is not one concerning monuments. "Our scale is small," he said. "We're not trying to be big. We're trying to use the resources of the small-town environment." The Owen Block conversion is an appropriate example of how New Harmony is carrying out that idea.

Main Street, New Harmony: human scale and a coherent streetscape.

An early rendering of the Winooski Block, showing its importance as a center of activity.

Gilding the Eagle on the Block Highlights a Different Urban Renewal Strategy

Winooski Block   Winooski, Vermont

Across the river from Burlington, the Winooski Block commands the entrance into Winooski, a once thriving mill town now staging a comeback from the urban renewal bulldozer. The restoration of this elaborate local landmark serves as a catalyst for the renovation of remaining buildings and encourages compatible infill construction. It is also enabling Winooski craftsmen to exercise their ample skills, just as they did when the block was first constructed.

Built in 1967, the Winooski Block exemplifies the wealth and exuberance of New England mill towns at that time. Three prominent local businessmen engaged Burlington architect Warren Thayer to raise a large commercial block in the popular High Italianate style. All the materials were crafted locally: the bricks were fired at Francis Le Clair's brickyard, the iron window sills and caps were cast at the Edwards and Stevens Foundry, and the bracketed wooden cornice was crowned by a five-foot-tall gilt eagle, hand carved from a single block of wood.

Like many commercial buildings of its day, the Winooski Block served a va-

riety of commercial and community functions. Its prominent location at the corner of East Allen and Main Streets attracted many small businesses, and to this day a hardware store and a corner pharmacy have occupied portions of the ground floor. On the top floor, a 60-by-53-foot concert hall housed the

town's French and English-speaking Catholic congregations until they were able to build their own churches. The hall was best known as the home of Sherman's Cornet Band, which gave free outdoor concerts in Winooski's Mill Park before moving to larger quarters in Burlington.

As the town's fortunes faded in the mid-twentieth century, so did the appearance of the Winooski block. Shabby storefront renovations cloaked the elegant ground floor details, and the upper two stories were broken up into a warren of shabby apartments. Winooski, like so many other towns, used its urban renewal funds to demolish many of the surrounding commercial buildings in 1973. Isolated atop a hill, the Winooski Block stood as a poignant reminder of what once had been a flourishing downtown district.

In 1978, the owners of the building approached the non-profit Winooski Community Development Corporation about funds for restoring the facade and renovating the interior apartments. WCDC director Mark Tigan saw the project as an effective way to create a new ethic for redevelopment in Winooski, in direct contrast to the methods of the early seventies.

From the outset, the WCDC attempted to recall Winooski's 19th-century days of prosperity by restoring the building and the surrounding area to its original character. Tigan hired townscape planner Ronald Lee Fleming and his public interest planning organization in Cambridge, along with architect Martin Tierney of Burlington.

Before restoration, the block is run down. Typical storefront changes contribute to the seedy appearance.

The brick has been cleaned and repainted, the lettering restored and the eagle recarved. New, modest Aubuchon Hardware sign respects visual character of the building.

Many wooden and cast iron elements had deteriorated beyond repair and had to be recarved or recast to match the originals. As in 1867, local craftsmen were called in for the work. The eagle was completely redone by Jim Young of Burlington, using cypress wood recycled from brewery vats in New York that were bolted together and carved over a three-week period. Though it was Moose Creek's first restoration project, the quality of their work on the Winooski Block has spawned other restoration projects in the area by resuscitating old skills. When the Winooski eagle sat once more atop its elaborate cornice, it was as if Winooski's workers had equalled the efforts of their ancestors.

CONTEXT

The restoration of the Winooski Block, long considered the most significant Victorian office block in Vermont, creates an interesting counterpoint of two styles of urban renewal. On the bare slope below it, cleared some years ago with urban renewal funds, stands a recently constructed shopping mall. It, too, is brick and tries, in the repetition of arched forms, to relate to the 19th-century mills below it on the river. Only after considerable attention had been paid to the old structures that survived the clearance—such as the Winooski Block—was the deal consummated with developers. Of course, proximity to burgeoning Burlington and the increasing Canadian investment in Vermont have also supported the rehabilitation of two large mills into housing and a riverfront park; but it is the reaffirmation of value in the old buildings which is helping the city put the pieces back together.

Fleming's group developed guidelines and a successful application for funds from the state preservation office, while the Tierney firm prepared drawings for the renovation. The $140,000 project, using mostly federal funds, was divided into two sections: cleaning and restoration of the paint, brickwork, and cast iron detailing on the upper stories; and restoration of the original storefronts. Moose Creek Restoration of Burlington was hired for the restoration work, completed in 1980.

When scaffolding was erected, it became apparent that the masonry was in a state of advanced deterioration, and that the original facade had been painted salmon pink. This stirred a minor controversy: a good sealant was needed to prevent further spalling of the brick, and since none was available, it would have to be painted. The WCDC

wanted salmon pink, but many townspeople found this a little *too* historically accurate. They wanted a more natural color.

The new eagle on the block.

Before restoration: a crumbling facade and a missing eagle, surrounded by the vacant lots of urban renewal.

An Eagle Soars Again Despite Downtown Demolition Follies

Detroit Cornice and Slate   Detroit, Michigan

Detroit is not a city traditionally acclaimed for its great strides in the field of architectural preservation. Lindburgh's birthplace, Union Depot, Old City Hall and a host of other architecturally significant buildings now survive only in photographs and memories, replaced in most cases by parking lots. But the Detroit Cornice and Slate Building is encouraging evidence that the City has taken a turn for the better. The distinctive facade, surmounted by an imposing metal eagle and now immaculately restored, is a lone but proud survivor of Detroit's urban renewal.

This High Victorian Italianate building was erected in 1897 for the founder of Detroit Cornice and Slate, Frank Hesse. Designed by Henry J. Rill, the three-story facade is an exceptional example of the use of galvanized steel, a material then becoming popular as an alternative to the more costly cast iron. Sheet metal was particularly well-re-

ceived in cities such as Detroit that lacked stone quarries, since the zinc-coated steel (like cast iron) could be painted to resemble cut stone. This trompe l'oeil effect was so successful in the case of Detroit Cornice and Slate that the City originally thought the building was stone and assessed it as such.

The intricate detailing in the facade's friezes and tympanums emulates stone carving and contributes to the building's ebullience. The detailing is actually hammered metal, and the work was done by hand in the very shop of Detroit Cornice and Slate, primarily a roofing business. Atop the crowning pediment of the facade was a zinc eagle, 150 pounds in weight, that in the words of one commentator cast a "defiant gaze" over the east side of the City.

The Detroit Cornice and Slate Company occupied the building continuously for seventy-four years and made

no architectural additions or alterations to the facade. As the Company expanded it finally found its downtown site too small and, in 1972, moved to a suburb. The vacant building passed to Frank Hesse's daughter Aurelia Voller, who had little use for the structure but "just didn't feel right about selling it" to see it demolished like its neighbors. Voller had fond memories of the building; her uncle had worked there as well as her father, and for years she and her seven brothers and sisters had gone there every day for lunch. For the next three years the building was vacant and unused, but, at least, still standing.

The building was saved by Tony and Maggie Citrin, who drove by one day in 1975 and immediately were attracted by its possibilities. Citrin, partner in a family real estate investment firm, soon arranged to buy the building. Thanks to the Citrins' efforts, the building's continued life was assured; eventually both Detroit's Common Council and the State of Michigan designated Detroit Cornice and Slate as an historic landmark.

The Citrins hired the architecture firm of William Kessler and Associates to investigate preserving the building. Kessler's discoveries were encouraging: he reported that the existing structure was sound and that the preservation of the building would save materials, time, and money.

Although the ornate facade had originally been galvanized to prevent deterioration, it had rusted over the years—"about thirty-five or forty percent," William Kessler estimated. Parts of the facade needed to be patched, while others needed to be entirely re-formed. After a long search, Kessler found Ed Semick, whom he pronounced "one of the few craftsmen left in this world," in a downtown body shop. Semick and an assistant spent over three months cleaning, patching and rehammering much of the original metal, and recreating the missing parts of the facade based on what was there or what could be symmetrically derived. New parts were bolted into place on the cleaned facade. The finished metal work was painted with an oil-base paint containing silica, giving the facade once again the appearance of stone. The remaining three brick walls of the building were then cleaned, the window openings remaining the same while single plates of glass replaced the older sash windows.

The original eagle had been stolen

34

during the 1950's, and the supply of ornamental eagles with six-foot wing spans is not particularly large in Detroit. Nevertheless, after much searching another one was finally located. Amidst a crowd of cheering people and helium balloons, the antique replacement eagle was raised to the roof, symbolically heralding the resurrection of this exceptional building.

CONTEXT

Today the Detroit Cornice and Slate Building houses a restaurant, artist's studio, and the offices of William Kessler and Associates. Once part of a thriving commercial district, it stands alone amidst parking lots, its sparkling facade a testament to the value of skillful restoration and an incentive, one hopes, to further restoration efforts in Detroit. It has been acclaimed by several architectural and building magazines.

Writing about the health of preservation efforts in Detroit, Edward D. Francis of William Kessler and Assoicates called the situation still "extremely depressing." He added, though, that preservation activity is growing in strength, and concluded that "hopefully, the tragedies of the past will not be repeated to such a great extent in the future." The eagle's "defiant gaze," now levelled at the results of urban renewal, will perhaps see to that.

A stirring reminder of the benefits of preservation that Detroit will do well to heed. There's still plenty of room for parking. (Photo by Balthazar Korab)

A Drug Facade Embalmed Under Glass is Resurrected

Ecker Drug Store   Corning, New York

"One of the greater sins of modernization" is how the National Trust's *Preservation News* described the 1965 project that enshrouded the Ecker Drug Store in slick, contemporary panelling. The subsequent removal of those same panels was heralded by the *Preservation News*, residents of Corning, and also the Market Street Restoration Agency, which considered this dramatic reversal a symbol of their progress in rehabilitating Corning's entire main street.

The Ecker Drug Store was built in 1885 by the architect E. B. Gregory. Generous in proportion, the three-story brick building features broad recessed arches and decorative inserts. The center of the facade was originally accentuated by a roofline cornice projection, intended to further the somewhat imposing image of its corner location. Retail shops have always occupied the ground floor and, aside from the modernization of the corner shop in 1913, the building remained essentially unchanged for its first eighty years.

In 1965, the decision by Ecker's owner to renovate the facade coincided with the desire of the Corning Glass Works to test the success of a new panelling material. The result: the instal-lation of "pyroceram" panels that covered all of the Ecker building but the ground floor level. Significant cosmetic and structural alterations were made to the building in order to attach the panels and to create a compatible modern image for the exposed ground floor. At the roofline, the cornice was entirely removed to create a flush surface for mounting. The sidestreet display window and the smaller rear windows on that side were blocked, structural piers were removed and replaced with I-beams, the two-story building next door was annexed, and the common wall between the two sections was also supported by an I-beam. The brick of the ground floor was covered over by a stone aggregate, epoxied onto the brick surface.

For fifteen years the building sported this slick surface, undoubtedly intended to emulate that of the new suburban stores. As noted by one Corning observer, however, Ecker's had become a visually negative space. "It was

35

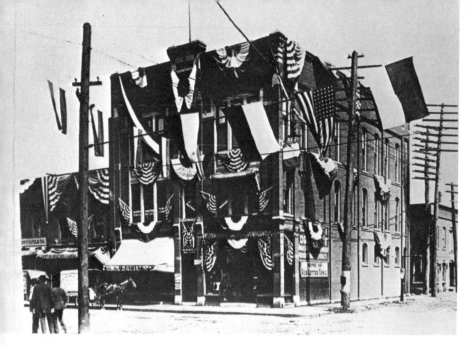

Ca. 1895. There is a clear orientation toward Market Street.

a non-building, the 1960s denial of historic buildings," says Harvey Kaplan, former staff designer for the Market Street Restoration Agency, Inc. (MSRA). The MSRA had renovated several facades on Main Street since its inception in 1974. Since Ecker's was a large building and the alterations were so egregious, the MSRA considered its restoration particularly important. In 1978, they obtained a $13,291 federal matching grant from the Heritage Conservation and Recreation Service of the U.S. Department of the Interior, with the Corning Glass Works and Ecker's owners meeting that figure. Work soon began to remove the panels and redress the underlying damage.

In several places the MSRA had to rebuild missing or damaged pieces. The stepped brick cornice was totally reconstructed, and several of the cast stone decorative elements were replaced. The ground floor posed the greatest problem, since the stone aggregate remained securely epoxied; the MSRA decided to simply leave the stone in place, allowing for the future development of removal methods, and to paint the stone surface to match the brick. Windows on the ground floor were opened, the facade was chemically cleaned, and awnings were installed to approximate the original appearance and to soften the contrast between the still-modern first floor door and windows and the original upper levels. The building today houses a gift shop and home health center as well as Ecker's Drug Store.

CONTEXT

Founded on the Chemung River as the center of a lumber region in 1835, the town of Corning remained small until a glass company from Brooklyn relocated there in 1868. This burgeoning company, which took the town's name to become the Corning Glass Works, continued to grow and inspired a building boom that produced the handsome four-block Market Street. The Corning Glass Works became the mainstay of the town and, although the older commercial buildings remained standing, by 1960 suburban development had lured the majority of residential and commercial activity away from downtown Corning. More than sixty bars lined Market Street, and employees of the Glass Works looked upon the town as little more than a parking lot and a watering hole.

A 1970 urban renewal plan for the town, partially funded by the Corning Glass Works (CGW) Foundation, originally called for eight square blocks of new downtown development, but this plan was aborted in 1972 when new president Thomas Buechner took hold of an idea that two Corning women had been advocating for several years: renovating, not demolishing, the historic Market Street. The CGW Foundation then provided a grant to support the development of this second plan, which sought instead to re-establish Market Street as an attractive commercial center and also as a downtown mecca for the thousands of visitors who annually

"A non-building, the 1960's denial of historic buildings." There is no orientation toward the street, and the building is uninviting to the pedestrian.

Ecker Drug as found. The cornice, pediment, and column ornamentation had been stripped away during installation of the pyroceram panels. At the right, architect's inscription stone has somehow survived.

Ecker Drug as restored. Decorative elements have been reconstructed, but the epoxied aggregate on the ground floor columns cannot be removed. Awnings help to obscure this jarring element.

tour the Corning Glass Center. This plan, too, was disrupted, by Hurricane Agnes, which caused the Chemung River to flood more than sixty percent of the town. The hurricane did considerable damage, yet in bringing federal disaster funds to the town to be used for new sidewalks and trees, it may have served as a catalyst uniting the town in the effort to rebuild and rehabilitate.

With a $64,000 grant from the CGW Foundation, the Market Street Restoration Agency was founded in 1974 in response to the increasing need for downtown design guidance. Under the direction of preservation advocate Norman Mintz, the agency provides free design education and advice while building owners and merchants pay for actual construction. Most of the Market Street projects are small in scope and inexpensive, and the occasional larger projects such as Ecker's have received supplementary funding.

It is this attention to the educational and low-cost aspects of rehabilitation, as well as the presence of a fulltime director, that have made the MSRA's endeavor successful and have prompted similar groups from all over the country to incorporate the Corning concepts within their own programs. Over seventy-five percent of Corning's merchants and property owners have participated in the MSRA program, and this visible improvement combined with comprehensive advertising and promotion has drawn many shoppers back into Market Street. But, writes Norman Mintz, equally important as the economic benefits of the Market Street rehabilitation is "the newfound pride that the community now has for *their* downtown."

Unfettered Facades Encourage a New Eagle to Roost

Market Street Emporium   Portsmouth, New Hampshire

These five brick buildings on Portsmouth's historic Market Street had been bound in white vinyl siding by a new tenant in 1968. Ten years later, the owner began restoring them to their original Federal appearance as part of a larger preservation effort in the city's waterfront section.

Constructed between 1815 and 1820, after Portsmouth's great fire of 1813, this block of five brick buildings on Market Street saw few changes until the 1890's. In 1895, the buildings were modernized by the addition of cast iron columns and large display windows, and the taller four-story buildings were gutted and replaced inside by three more spacious stories. The block consisted of adjacent but independently-operated retail shops, including hardware, furniture and clothing concerns.

A local merchant, George Kimball, purchased five of these stores in 1954 and established a large women's wear and department store that occupied all five of them. He operated Kimball's for more than a decade before leasing it to D. Lynch and Company of Manchester, New Hampshire. Although the firm retained the well-known Kimball's name, the Lynch managers decided to give the store a new image. At a cost of $20,000 in 1968, the stores were enveloped in white vinyl siding and the storefronts were once again modernized. All of the display windows were

37

Market Street ca. 1920. The five stores on the far right (leading back to the triangular pediment) were later to become Kimball's.

lowered, and the storefronts were made to look uniform by the addition of identical brick columns that covered over the older granite and cast iron. An oversized pseudocolonial pediment hung uncomfortably over the new glass and aluminum main entrance doors. If the goal of the Lynch Company was to create a massive impact on the street, it is undeniable that these alterations fulfilled their purpose.

By 1978, falling sales had discouraged the Lynch Company from renewing their lease. Owner George Kimball then resumed management of the Market Street block. Encouraged by other restoration work in the Portsmouth area, Kimball decided to remove the vinyl siding from the buildings. He approached Portsmouth's City Planning Office, which has a free-of-charge consultation service, and enlisted the help of planner Paul Gosselin. The two devised a plan to make the several buildings work together as a mini-mall.

The first rehabilitation step was the removal of the vinyl siding at a cost of $2,000, and Kimball was able to sell both the siding and the supporting two-by-four-foot plywood sheets at a profit. Once the storefronts were exposed, Gosselin could see the extent to which they had been altered and decide how best to proceed. The window display area had suffered the greatest damage: the cast iron framing members had been severed, and the windows no longer extended to their original height.

Because Kimball wanted to keep the exterior renovation cost as low as possible, Gosselin decided to keep the dropped windows and the flanking brick columns, but he chose to retain and accentuate the older cast iron segments as well. He created new panelling in the clerestory section of the windows, recalling the proper height of the storefronts, and painted the cast iron light green.

Additional work included the installation of new windows and doors—he discovered the old walnut doors of two stores in the basements and reinstalled them—and rehabilitation of the upper stories to office and residential space. The modern glass and aluminum main entrance doors were retained, again for cost reasons. Although visually it would be preferable to install more compatible entrance doors, remove the brick columns, exposing the underlying cast iron, and return the windows and framing members to their original proportions, Gosselin's solution is acceptable given the budget constraints; the exterior renovations for the entire block cost less than $20,000. Furthermore, this work could serve as the basis for a more complete restoration in the future.

An exceptional feature of this project is the Market Street Emporium entrance sign, with its carved gilded eagle. George Kimball personally researched this aspect of the project in order to create an appropriate sign of the early nineteenth century. A similar sign had existed elsewhere in Portsmouth, and Kimball commissioned local craftsman, Steve McHenry, to work in the same medium: gold leaf lettering on a background of black paint mixed with sand, a technique known as schmaltz. The crowning Bellamy eagle is of an early local craftsman.

Aluminum siding, brick piers, and a pseudo-Colonial doorway. The facades have lost their character and uniqueness.

The stores are joined by this common entrance, but they are once again independently operated as The Classic Woman and D. Graham's, women's and men's clothing, respectively, and Here's How, linens and curtains. Harland's Leathers on the right-hand end of the block is now an independently-owned building as is G. Willikers, the toy store to the left.

CONTEXT

In the year 1630, a group of 80 English settlers disembarked on the shores of the Piscataqua River and, finding the embankments covered with wild strawberries, named their new settlement Strawbery Banke. The town later changed its name to Portsmouth and flourished on seaborne commerce for more than two centuries, until the advent of the railroads in the late 1800s. As the timber and shipbulding trades died, a new generation of European immigrants moved in and converted many of the homes and warehouses to multi-family dwellings. The old waterway was filled in and gradually overrun with junkyards, and by the 1950s the area was marked for urban renewal demolition.

Federal money was used for a massive clearance just north of Market Street, which received much local criticism. In the south end of the city, a group of citizens proposed the revolutionary idea of using urban renewal funds for historic preservation. Their support saved the neighborhood and led to the formation of Strawbery Banke, Inc., a preservation organization dedicated to conserving this ten-acre section of 17th and 18th-century Portsmouth.

The increased awareness of the city's architectural heritage that started in Strawbery Banke spread to the waterfront area and adjacent downtown commercial district, sparking a "townscape plan" commissioned by the City Planning Office and prepared by Ronald Lee Fleming and a team of architects. The plan, which was produced at a time of increasing national disenchantment with urban renewal, respected the character of the existing city. Individual merchants participated in design clinics held by the townscape team, who produced drawings of how particular buildings had looked and could look again. These clinics initiated a reappraisal of many downtown properties and supported the eventual

The new Market Street Emporium, replete with golden eagle. Removal of the aluminum siding has revealed the 1895 cast iron mullions at the clerestory level, along with the Federal style facade above. Signs fit in well with proportion and style, but the thick brick piers by the doorway are still disconcerting. Williker's (to the right) and Harland's (to the left) have restored facades as a result of Kimball's effort.

decision of George Kimball to rediscover his Market Street facades.

Federal funds were later employed in Portsmouth to landscape the historic downtown market square and improve pedestrian amenities. Private business ventures further contributed to the success of the district, as a revival of husband-and-wife-operated businesses developed. The Market Street Emporium is the most dramatic example of the new business attitude in the city, one in which merchants are less interested in large-scale franchises than in the management and the appearance of their own particular buildings.

Big Boy Grows Up to Accept Cityscape Responsibility

Elias Brothers' Big Boy   Traverse City, Michigan

A town without the protection of historic district ordinances is usually an architectural pushover for a franchise with a legacy of standardized facades. The Beadle Building in Traverse City is a rare example of a fast-food operation that restored a building facade to a likeness of its original appearance. This fortuitous development was engineered by a preservation-conscious citizenry and economic development corporation.

In 1978, Big Boy acquired a property on West Front Street known as the Beadle Building. The building was constructed in the late 1880's of Graelickville common brick, a white, soft brick used frequently at that time in the Grand Traverse Bay region. Originally it was a moderate-sized but ornate building, with a central triangular pediment, pressed iron railing along the roofline, and decorative arches of cast

The Beadle Building in 1905. Triangular pediment, decorative pressed iron on roof, and cast iron columns on ground floor are no longer there.

concrete over the second-story windows. A photograph from the turn of the century reveals that the Beadle Building formerly had cast iron one-story columns framing the display windows as well as a low veranda with a sloping roof extending over the sidewalk.

The building was used for retail business, and over the years the facade was altered as the businesses changed. By the 1950's the pediment and ornamental iron railing had disappeared, and a central doorway divided the facade into two dissimilar parts. During the 1960s the building was occupied by a drug store, and though the second story was relatively unaltered the ground floor was sheathed in vertical siding and was separated from the upper part of the building by a "hula skirt" of cedar shingles. This was the appearance of the Beadle Building when Elias Brothers' Big Boy purchased it in 1978.

Big Boy needed to convert the interior retail space into a restaurant and desired to renovate the exterior as well. In order to secure funding for the work, the franchise made a presentation to the Grand Traverse County Economic Development Corporation (EDC); the facade they proposed utilized the cedar

shakes and plastic common to corporate design. Several members of the EDC were, however, sensitive to the appearance of the City's downtown, and they declined to vote—thus refusing funding—on Big Boy's proposal. These members suggested that the franchise might instead attempt to restore the building and that if Big Boy were to do so, the EDC would be more interested in offering funding.

This economic incentive convinced Big Boy to seek out the services of Jeffry Corbin, a Traverse City designer who had already rehabilitated several other commercial buildings. Corbin drew up a new facade proposal, and when Big Boy returned to the EDC they were successful in securing $500,000 in financing. Of this amount, $110,000 was used for building acquisition and approximately $40,000 covered the cost of the new storefront.

Corbin's design involved a synthesis of old and new. He began by stripping the facade of its 1960's accretions—the shingled pseudo-roof, vertical siding, and window signs—and creating an uncluttered look. By relocating the entrance to the right-hand side, Corbin allowed for an unbroken expanse of display windows and necessary access

control for the restaurant. Thick vertical framing members and thinner horizontals create a pattern based on the Beadle Building's early appearance, but new unpainted wood was substituted for the cast iron columns and the glass used was solar-treated bronze. At the corners of the facade, brick posts have replaced the columns; the brick matches the original since it was obtained by reopening windows along the building's east side. Corbin also replaced the vertical band of bricks above the display windows. The original facade had utilized a saw-toothed band of half-round bricks but, since half-round bricks could not be found at a reasonable price, he substituted straight brick with the same saw-tooth characteristic. One other decorative element, the pressed iron grillwork along the roofline, is being remade in aluminum. Since the triangular pediment would cost $10,000 to re-create, it was deemed too poor a return on investment to warrant replacing.

Jeffry Corbin has re-created the facade's early liveliness particularly through his use of color: the cast concrete panels and roof cornice are painted blue, the long sign is maroon with gold typography, and the inset

"Beadle building" panel has been highlighted in gold leaf on deep blue. The building is consequently eye-catching and has been popular with residents. Big Boy's business has exceeded original estimates, perhaps because of this polished design. Corbin notes that late-nineteenth century architecture can be very "human oriented, visually stimulating, and colorfully sensitive" when properly renovated, and that he has been amazed by the number of positive comments from the general public to this project and other Traverse City renovations carried out by his office.

CONTEXT

Located at the mouth of the Grand Traverse Bay of Lake Michigan, Traverse City was settled around 1850 as a lumbering town; by the twentieth century, its economic base had shifted to fruit growing and tourism. Traverse City has continued to grow and industrialize, but the overall feeling is still of a "big small town." Local residents still shop primarily in the downtown area, and as a result of their patronage and the sensitivity of the Economic Development Commission, the downtown district has not been overlooked in recent planning studies. The objectives of the current city plan include retaining quality historical commercial structures, designing new buildings compatible in scale and quality, and encouraging storefront renovations that highlight original forms. Traverse City is fortunate to have a large proportion of residents who care about where and how they live more than money-making development schemes. One resident commented that he could undoubtedly earn a better living elsewhere, but chose to stay in Traverse City where "the view of the Bay is part of the pay." Under the watchful eyes of such residents, Traverse City will probably continue to negotiate firmly with the franchises, whose marketing sophistication acknowledges the benefits of attractive locations while their facade design often erodes it. In this case, Big Boy's design sensitivity was encouraged to mature to compatible adulthood.

In 1979, with "hula skirt" of cedar shingles and covered ground floor facade.

The Big Boy franchise. Entrance has been moved to the left, wood columns replace cast iron. Brick corner piers match original brick, and saw-toothed decoration has been restored. Graphics are clear but unassuming. Color is important: blue decoration on upper story, maroon-and-gold sign above stained wood columns.

41

III · **Facades Adapted:** *New Uses for New Times*

As changing times demand new uses from downtown buildings, many facades are forced to adapt in order to survive. The facades in this chapter have survived in various stages of completeness—from the doorway slice of the CFC Building in Washington, D.C. to the expanded facade of the East Cambridge Savings Bank—by adapting with the structures behind them to serve different functions. Such facades in their altered state still serve as a sort of armature binding the memory of a past posture to a new use or condition. As a result, they provide a support for memory and new uses.

Often such a change calls for contemporary additions that bring essential functions into an older structure. A modern elevator tower enabled the architects to save half of the handsome but derelict Alamo Hotel in Colorado Springs, while an ingenious five-foot addition, scaled to match the original facade, assisted the restored Hendley Building in Galveston meet modern safety codes. In the case of the old Santa Cruz County Courthouse, a new side entrance and lush landscaping helped the building to alter its demeanor and put on a lively new face opening on an outdoor downtown mall. Soundproofing, addition of a third floor, and sealing of entries were all necessary to transform the old Rainbow Garage in San Francisco to its new role as a high school gymnasium and classroom building. In this case a restrained treatment of the building facade aided the high school in overcoming neighborhood opposition.

Sometimes, though, modern adaptations of old buildings stir controversies over the respect given to the original facades. In Granbury, Texas, First National Bank's creation of a downtown drive-through facility by punching through the ground floor of a neighboring facade may have served a role in keeping business downtown, but viewed up close it seems a less satisfactory design solution. The new Museum of Natural History in Louisville housed in rehabilitated warehouse buildings, also supported downtown revitalization, but the architect's placement of a second facade of shiny aluminum behind the elegant cast iron original prompted serious debate about whether new design should accommodate pedestrians or automobiles in such an area. The recessed entry scooped into the Maud Building facade in Seattle, to light a basement restaurant was considered so detrimental to the building's character that the city's Historic District Commission changed its policy on permitting recesses in historic facades. And the architectural plaudits for the addition to the East Cambridge Savings Bank's ornate facade obscured the controversy over two historic townhouses pulled down to accommodate additional parking for the expansion.

The adaptable faces in this chapter owe at least part of their resilience to the characteristics of earlier facade design. Their formal organization into a symmetry of elements and a hierarchical arrangement of forms allows them to be subtracted or added to while still retaining their dignity. Since they do not attempt to explain the structural integrity of the structures behind them, these facades can be separated from their buildings, sometimes more tactfully than at other times. Sociologist Richard Sennett has suggested that modern facades are "history-proof" because they cannot adapt in this way; the rigid adherence of the facade to expressing the structure makes it useless without that structure. It is possible, then, that the facades documented in this chapter will continue to adapt and will survive long after some of their modern neighbors have become obsolescent.

Classic Facade Helps Neighborhood Accept Conversion From Garage to Gymnasium

San Francisco University High School   San Francisco, California

A change of uses often engenders local opposition, especially in residential neighborhoods. When San Francisco's University High School proposed expanding into the unused Rainbow Garage in 1977, the genteel Pacific Heights neighborhood and its political allies raised a storm of protest. Acknowledgement of the community's interests and a respectful renovation helped the project go through—and the high school has turned out to be a very good neighbor.

The two-story poured concrete Rainbow Garage, which is well-scaled to its residential surroundings, was constructed in 1922 to answer the immediate need for off-street automobile parking in a city recently risen from the rubble of the great San Francisco Earthquake. The facade is symmetrically divided into five bays—two exit, two entrance and one service—and is decorated with understated neo-Classic plaster ornamentation.

The Rainbow Garage served the quiet, well-to-do Washington Street neighborhood for fifty-three years. Although structurally sound, the peeling paint, gas station graphics, and crumbling ornamentation made it an eyesore. In 1975, the garage was sold to the University High School, which needed additional classrooms and a gymnasium to supplement existing facilities located across the street. Neighborhood residents were apprehensive about the proposed expansion of the high school; not only would they lose valuable parking space, but students, they feared, would be even noisier than a service garage. Beneath this layer of concern was the more subtle problem of resentment concerning public-versus-private education.

Local protest was spearheaded by neighborhood resident Diane Feinstein, a member of the Finance Committee of the Board of Supervisors, which was so important to the budget-hungry Planning Commission. The Planning Commission's opposition to the project in turn sparked a wave of public support in which the school received 444 cards and 28 letters. A tumultuous public hearing was held by the Planning Commission and at the final vote, 200 spectators were present to witness the 4–2 vote in favor of the High School.

Although the High School addition was finally granted a building permit, the permit was given conditionally: the school was to be well soundproofed and visually integrated with its neighbors by careful attention to window glazing, color treatment, and other exterior improvements.

The old Rainbow Garage: a restrained Neoclassical facade, including masks and medallions, for a genteel neighborhood.

Architect James E. Palmer, who was dedicated to championing the acceptance of the University High School addition, forged an attractive, practical building from the old garage. In accordance with the restrictions placed on the building by the Planning Commission, the interior of the High School featured acoustically dampened walls, ceilings and floors and double glazed windows on the upper gymnasium floor.

The crumbling facade was scraped and the deteriorating plaster mouldings and ornamentation recast by local craftsmen. Palmer re-painted the red, white and blue facade in color-coordinated shades of unobtrusive earth green which fit well into the residential neighborhood. Filling in certain doorways and windows of the facade in order to strengthen the walls, Palmer left the openings as niches in order to pre-

Though windows and garage entrances have been covered to create just one doorway, keeping the recesses maintains rhythm of the bays. Mansard roof slopes back unobtrusively. Earth green color fits into streetscape better and brings out decorative elements. With new face and new planting, building makes better use of its site, and the gymnasium functions are not obvious.

serve the original facade rhythm. The acoustically dampened new "mansard" roof was sloped back from the existing parapet to prevent it from obtruding on the predominantly two-story streetscape. New sidewalks and planting in keeping with the other planting on the street, completed the respectable transformation of the old Rainbow Garage.

CONTEXT

The San Francisco University High School has turned out to be a handsome addition to the residential neighborhood. The transformation of the run-down garage into an attractive institution has increased property values, and in general the renovation is well accepted. Writes architect Palmer:

The building has shown that the

school is a concerned and 'good' neighbor, responsive to community interests and to the growing need to improve and enhance urban lifestyles—not by discarding the past but by integrating it into the fabric of our ever-changing times.

Diane Feinstein is now the mayor of San Francisco, and finds the renovation totally acceptable.

A Controversial Double Facade
Splits a Vision of Past and Future

Louisville Museum of Natural History   Louisville, Kentucky

Louisville's Museum of Natural History building presents a controversial juxtaposition of old and new in a double facade: an 1878 cast iron frontispiece and a sleek aluminum front constructed one hundred years later. While the new museum has sparked vitality in an old downtown district, the building itself raises an important question: Is there a single appropriate preservation approach?

The Carter Dry Goods building, largest of five old buildings which the museum occupies, proclaims its origin on a cast iron plaque flanking the entrance: "C.J. Clarke, Arch and Snead and Bibb, ironworks." The nineteenth century tobacco magnate who financed the building named it "The Two Sisters" in honor of his two granddaughters. When Carter Dry Goods opened its doors, the first two floors of the three-bay building catered to the public while the remaining four stories served as a warehouse for company stock. As the business expanded, the entire building was converted to a warehouse; between 1895 and 1908 the original three bays were expanded to seven.

It remained a warehouse until 1972, when a commercial redevelopment company bought the building and started renovations, intending to include it and adjoining structures in an arcade of small shops. After spending $40,000 to remove the fire escape, repaint the trim and sandblast the brick, the company halted renovations due to economic difficulties. The Carter Dry

Goods building fell vacant and unused; it was protected from demolition only because it stood in an area which had

been proclaimed a local historic district in 1974 and was itself on the National Register.

Meanwhile, Louisville searched for a museum site. In 1960 citizens had approved a $600,000 bond issue for a

The old Carter Dry Goods building in 1973, in desperate need of restoration.

44

Museum of Natural History intended to feature local flora, fauna, geography and industry, and since then a succession of mayors had fruitlessly proposed different sites. The mayor in 1972, Harvey Sloane, an advocate of urban revitalization, favored a downtown site for the museum. Sloane convinced the city to use the bond issue to buy the Carter Dry Goods building and the four buildings adjoining it. He argued that the downtown site would be near parking and hotel facilities, as well as near the Falls of the Ohio River, which had played a major role in Louisville's development and could be the theme of the museum. In addition, the Carter Dry Goods building was near a Devonian Ledge on the Falls, a geological formation which could provide opportunities for the museum-sponsored nature studies.

In order to fund the museum, the city raised a total of $5.3 million from various public and private sources. Sloane rushed the project, well aware of the probability that the museum plan would be changed by a successor. Before HUD had approved its one-half share of the funding, construction had already started on Jeffrey Point's dramatic design which incorporated industrial materials into an old framework. When Louisville's Museum of Natural History opened on July 4, 1977, the building, as much as the exhibits, was on display.

Considered to be one of Louisville's best cast iron buildings, the five-story Carter Dry Goods facade incorporates the iron with limestone and sandstone in a unified design. The segmental arches are embellished with panels decorated with incised vines and each arch opening is separated by applied pilasters and Corinthian columns of red sandstone.

Jeffrey Points, of the firm Louis and Henry, retained the Carter Dry Goods facade design with slight but significant changes. He created a sixteen-foot deep entryway space by removing floor sections from the first two stories and exposed the facade on both sides thus isolating it as a 'landmark'. Then behind the rectilinear iron and stone Carter Dry Goods facade, he placed a new facade, which sweeps in and out toward the original front in sheer curves of vented aluminum.

Both the materials and the design of the new facade intend to contrast with the older building. Whereas the old fa-cade is intricate and, to some extent, handmade, the new facade seems to be industrially mass-produced—even though it is in fact custom-fabricated interlocking strips of anodized aluminum.

The interior of the museum continues this striking old-new juxtaposition: a dramatic five-story interior atrium pierces through the Carter Dry Goods building, letting in natural light and exposing much of the original column grid. Next to exposed duct work are original brick walls; near corrugated aluminum elevator shafts are original cast iron columns. And industrial pipe railings guide visitors through all eighteen original levels of the new-old building.

CONTEXT

The Louisville Museum of Natural History was, in the words of Louisville Landmarks Commission Executive Director Ann Hassett, "the single largest shot in the arm for the whole Mainstreet area." The museum, along with other renovation projects in the downtown historic district, has drawn large numbers of people back into an area which was in dire economic straits only ten years ago. The success of the museum spawned other preservation activity in the area; as a result, property taxes have skyrocketed and there is much real estate speculation.

At the same time, the museum has generated a considerable amount of controversy in the architectural world. The forceful juxtaposition of old and new, a common design technique of the modern movement, has recently come under heavy criticism. Architectural critic William Morgan of the *Louisville Courier-Journal* accused Points of engaging in a "meaningless exercise in keeping up with the architectural Joneses." He criticized the removal of

Cleaning and pointing has brought out the elegance of the clustered columns, contrasting them with the anodized aluminum facade behind. Larger windows seem uncomfortable without mullions or glass.

the window mullions and panes, saying that the architect "demonstrated a lack of understanding of the nature of the 19th century commercial architecture in his interruption of the rhythm of the streetscape." Morgan also criticized the basic design concept of contrast, writing that "their new facade behind the old one, with its mirror surfaces, represents a slick exercise in a trendy 1920's revival style that is more appropriate to a fashionable discotheque than to the older structure which it joins and should visually support."

Others, however, argue that a meaninful relationship between old and new is in fact established by this juxtaposition. David Morton of *Progressive Architecture* writes that Points "has used a modern industrial material in the old industrial spaces, thereby creating an ambience of great sophistication that shares as much concern for the past as it does for the present."

Jeffrey Points responded to Morgan in a letter to the editor of the *Louisville Courier-Journal* writing that:

> . . . when the Carter Building was originally constructed, rhythm was more closely related to the pedestrian . . . driving by this same building today at 35 miles per hour in an air-conditioned vehicle, one perceives only a blur of this detail, but is still very aware of the overall larger scale rhythm by the columns and window arrangements which have been left intact.

To the assertion that his building materials are "more appropriate to a discotheque," Points replies that the comment has been taken as "a back-handed compliment. There was a very deliberate attempt to create the impression of fun, excitement and adventure in space to complement the dynamic programmatic concept of the museum."

Points and Morgan have the same goal: they both believe that a preservation technique should respect the integrity of an old building. But the architectural styles they think will achieve this goal are very different. Morgan affirms that the new construction should blend new and old unjarringly to evoke the flavor of the nineteenth century pedestrian-scaled building. Points, on the other hand, feels that both new and old construction are thrown into more plastic relief by their juxtaposition. Should compatibility contrast be the basis for a preservation strategy, that remains the question.

A Facade Slice Recalls a Past Street Orientation

CFC Square   Washington, D.C.

In another bold combination of new and old, CFC Square in Washington's historic Georgetown presents a thoroughly modern facade of brick, tile and glass except for a single and central bay of masonry enclosing a decorated limestone doorway. This fragment is not a "historicizing" addition but a remnant of the building's former identity, a testimony to the structure's humble beginnings as a warehouse in 1927.

In 1975 the National Rural Utilities Cooperative Finance Corporation (CFC), acquired a 57,000 square foot site between 29th and 30th streets and the C & O Canal. The site already contained a 25,000-square-foot neo-Georgian office building built in 1957, a 100,000-square-foot warehouse along the canal built in 1937, and a parking lot. CFC intended only to upgrade these basically sound structures to the mini-

The 1927 warehouse with the canal in the background. With main entrance here on 30th Street, building ignores the water.

Looking across the canal at the new facade of the CFC building. New floor reorients the structure toward the canal; facade slice on 30th Street recalls the past but seems overlooked.

mum extent necessary for conversion to comfortable office space. The parking lot was to be reserved for future and undefined expansion. A suit by Georgetown residents precipitated more ambitious plans. They objected to the encroaching commercialization of their exclusive neighborhood and demanded that the CFC site be rezoned as residential.

In response to this challenge, CFC considered the possibilities of accommodating their future neighbors while still putting the site to " a higher and better use." As zoning restrictions prevented immediate construction of more commercial office space, CFC decided to propose apartments. This served as a good transition to the adjoining residential neighborhood and appeased the community. Ironically, though Georgetown residents secured a definite commitment to residential use for part of the site, their actions pushed CFC to a more immediate and intensive development than might otherwise have occurred.

CFC chose as architect Arthur Cotton Moore, a native Washingtonian who had recycled many 19th century warehouses of this one-time tobacco port into what Wolf von Eckardt in the *New Republic* calls "architectural collages." At Canal Square, he remodelled an abandoned heavy timber and masonry warehouse and added 75,000 square feet of new construction to create a popular shopping, office, and eating enclave with underground parking. Across the C & O Canal at a corner to the CFC property, Moore renovated the old Duvall foundry into a terraced office building that emphasizes the water and the historic ironworks. The structure now contains a brick-paved plaza that hosts frequent concerts and celebrations, as well as serving as the home port for the National Park Service's mule-drawn canal barges.

Before approaching the warehouse facade, Moore first remodelled the 1957 office building to accommodate the CFC staff immediately. Its street facade left intact, the building was re-oriented to the future midblock plaza. A discreet addition provided a new lobby and an elevator tower. Beneath the remainder of the ground site is a parking garage, capped by the plaza from which the apartment building will rise. CFC has let "air rights" for this to a developer.

The south building, or the old warehouse, presents the most intriguing transformation. Hard-to-rent deep space was eliminated by reducing the warehouse's width, resulting in the loss of a considerable part of the north facade. This square footage was reassembled at

The old doorway contrasted with new brick facade.

47

the top of the building in the form of a fourth story and a penthouse floor. The existing warehouse exterior was "a melange of window types, patches of brick and concrete" resulting in what Moore calls "one of the ugliest buildings you ever did see." His response was to strip the building down to structural basics, recess the windows and reproportion the entire frame with a new brick and tile skin and special wood soffits. This transformation was comprehensive except for the one bay, the only aspect of the exterior that Moore thought possessed merit. Its heavy capped pediment frame, heraldic ornament on a brick ground, and crisply carved doorway give it a special identity. The element maintains the same relation with the rest of the building as it did previously, breaking slightly through the roofline and sitting asymmetrically on the front.

CONTEXT

Whereas the old warehouse shunned the canal, the new CFC building rediscovers the water. This change of focus is in keeping with the adjacent development up and down the waterway. The recent string of hotels, restaurants, shopping and office complex (many of them planned by Moore) have their principal face on the canal, which has been opened to the public through the creation of footpaths and amenities such as those at the Forge. It is thus unfortunate that the restaurant and outdoor cafe which Moore specified for the ground floor of the CFC building have not materialized. It would break up the blank face of the offices and provide some interaction between the building and pedestrians.

Moore wants the building to "tell the truth about its age." On 30th Street, it

does not obviously do so; the transition from the old fabric to the new is not seamless. The carved stone door is articulated by a new glass surrounding, which makes it a stronger focal point to compensate for the expansion of the new bays on either side.

The building is more explicit about its age and former function on the plaza side. Glass walls, ceiling coffering and lighting show off the old industrial mushroom capitol columns. While it may not be immediately recognizable as an old warehouse, the transformation does maintain the old familiar scale and relationships of the site. It resists, as Von Eckhardt recognizes, "the conventional, cataclysmic approach to urban revitalization." By admitting its age, even if reticently with only a facade slice, it preserves the resonances of an old building.

Half a Facade Helps a Derelict Building Make a Complete Recovery

Alamo Hotel   Colorado Springs, Colorado

The "search-and-destroy" method of urban renewal took a lot of fine old buildings from inner cities in the 1960's and 70's, when Colorado Springs was dutifully clearing parcels of downtown commercial property. The Alamo Hotel with its carefully articulated facade was next on the demolition list when some young developers stepped in to save it. Though they found that half the structure had to be demolished, they saved the remainder by attaching it to a contemporary brick tower. In doing so, they proved that half an old building can be better than many a new one.

The original Alamo Hotel was a wood frame structure built on this site around 1880, with a wing added to the north side about ten years later. Shortly thereafter, the main building burned and a new steel and concrete frame structure rose in its place. The old north wing was given a brick face lift to match the new construction, so that the building appeared to be a single structure with a central tower dominating the main facade.

The Alamo's facade was one of the jewels of Colorado Springs: a four story composition of Romanesque arches forming a symmetrical pattern around the central tower. Broad, low arches created large storefront display areas on the first floor, while tall, slender arches spanned the height of the middle two

The Alamo Hotel in 1905: a Romanesque Revival work with rounded arches, heavy stone beltcourses and decorated columns. Identical halves of front facade belie older woodframe construction of north section (to right). Side facade continues motif with less elegance.

By 1975, tower and side pediments have disappeared. Dirty stone and large signs reduce building's visual character.

floors. Paired columns inset in a loggia framed windows on the fourth floor, and a tall masonry cornice capped the building. Typical of this style were the strong horizontal belt courses and mouldings separating the first and fourth floors from the middle section.

Having served as a hotel for seventy years, the Alamo's life appeared to be over when the urban renewal authority called it "unsafe and unmarketable" in 1975 and slated it for demolition. A developer had already presented a proposal for a high-rise tower on the site but failed to secure financing at the last moment. Dave Barber and Gene Yergensen, two local architects, then joined with three other investors and submitted a renovation proposal.

"The Alamo was the last building standing in the renewal area," recalls Barber, "and it probably would have been torn down earlier if it weren't for the fact that it was serving as housing for the elderly and the city wanted to leave it up as long as possible." The developers offered to purchase the building for slightly more than the city's estimated demolition costs. Initially the city rejected the offer, as it had all previous renovation projects, but persistent negotiations—along with a lack of alternative offers—led to an agreement. The Alamo was purchased for $200,000, and construction began in 1976.

The architects knew they had one of the best facades left in town and wanted to preserve as much as possible. The old wood portion was severely dilapidated, however, and under pressure from the Building Department they had it removed. On the remaining half of the building, Barber and Yergensen had the brick cleaned and new windows installed. The north wall was patched where the old addition had been removed, and the entire wall painted to match the color of the finish brick on the main facade. New signs were fitted within the existing features, such as the arched entry, emphasizing the building's original details.

To make the Alamo succeed as an office building, the architects had to utilize as much interior space as possible. An elevator was needed for improved public access, but installing it within the building would have been difficult and expensive. The solution was to build a new tower to the south of the existing buildings, attached by a narrow glass bridge where the hotel balconies had been, so that no demolition was necessary to create connecting hallways. Originally, this tower was to have had a pseudo-Victorian cornice, but budget restrictions forced its elimination. Total project costs were $1.2 million.

CONTEXT

The Alamo lies on the southern edge of downtown; just to the south of it stands the historic courthouse (now a museum) and a new civic building. To the north and east, lots still lie vacant in the urban renewal area, but projects are now on the boards for these sites—

As restored in 1981. Old north section has been destroyed; as a result, south section is slightly unbalanced. Tower addition is somewhat stark, but it shows off the old structure by not competing and allows it to survive by incorporating essential functions. Glass wall at rear opens up to mountains in background; vacant lots of urban renewal are visible at the sides.

due in part to the success of the Alamo. "This handsome example of adaptive use encouraged other developers to do the same," says Elaine Freed, a leader in historic preservation in Colorado Springs. "It convinced a larger public of the economic value of renovation. It helped turn around the once fatalistic acceptance of a dying downtown." The Alamo was fully occupied within six months of renovation; today it houses a clothing store and restaurant on the ground floor, with E.F. Hutton and the Internal Revenue Service prominent among office tenants.

The Alamo stands out because of the barren surroundings and the revitalized aspects of its ornate facade, and it rarely fails to catch the attention of newcomers to the downtown. The modesty of the addition, built in identical brick, enhances the old structure, as it does not try to copy or compete with the old style. In the rear of the new tower, a glass wall opens up to spectacular views of nearby Pikes Peak.

Seven years ago, the Alamo was considered to be structurally unsound and unsalvageable. Barber and Yergensen proved this to be wrong and saved half of a beautiful building. By combining this half with a thoughtful contemporary addition, they have insured that the Alamo will serve useful functions for years to come.

Facade Turnabout Animates a Downtown Mall

Old County Courthouse   Santa Cruz, California

The imaginative redevelopment that saved the Old Santa Cruz County Courthouse is expressed by its facade change: from a single, somewhat stern entrance to a terraced, landscaped space opening onto an open garden mall around the corner from the original entrance. Renamed Cooper House, it is now an anchor of one of the more successful downtown revitalizations in the state.

Built in 1895 to a design by N. A. Comstock, the Courthouse is an imposing example of Richardsonian Romanesque, with its buff-colored brick and its foundation, arches, and gable ornament of carved grey sandstone. Its original tower was damaged and had to be removed after the 1906 San Francisco earthquake 75 miles to the north.

In 1968, the county government vacated the building in favor of a new "government center" nearby. For three years the old courthouse sat empty while its fate was discussed. The favored solution was to tear it down to provide all of nine additional parking spaces. Meanwhile, five blocks of Pacific Avenue (the town's main business street on the building's west) had been recently transformed through landscaping and facade renovations, in response to the construction of a new enclosed regional shopping center outside the town.

Chuck Abbott, a retired photographer who had spearheaded the "open garden mall" development, was concerned that the loss of the courthouse would be a serious blow to the historic character of Pacific Avenue. He persuaded the county to put the building up for a public auction, which it did—twice—with no takers. Undaunted, Mr. Abbott contacted Max Walden, who had recently completed a successful and acclaimed redevelopment of a former school building in nearby Los Gatos. Walden made a bid and purchased the building for $75,000. There was no stipulation in the contract for renovation on the part of the county; they were indifferent to its fate. But Walden stipulated a clause that the building could not be demolished in the next twenty years. He assumed (correctly) that by that time it would be thoroughly established as a community landmark and an economic success.

Walden basically followed the pattern he had previously established in Los Gatos. He developed spaces for a mix of about 20 shops, galleries, and restaurants, to take advantage of the building's location in an established commercial district as well as its proximity to the new University of California campus. Finding the building in sound structural condition, Walden made a few significant exterior alterations, all designed to reorient the building to Pacific Avenue. The courthouse had originally been built with a main, arched entrance on Cooper Street, named for the brothers who donated the land for it. Walden added a second entrance on Pacific Avenue for improved

The imposing old courthouse, showing main entrance on Cooper Street.

Cooper House logo, outdoor patio and landscaping enliven facade and tie it into garden mall on Pacific Avenue.

new regulations for renovation of historic structures.

The Pacific Gardens Mall is one of the more successful downtown redevelopments in California, transforming a depressed area into a lively shopping area. In contrast to the covered regional shopping malls, Pacific Avenue was designed to take advantage of Santa Cruz' mild climate with outdoor cafes and broad sidewalks. From the start, Cooper House was seen as an integral part of the mall, reflecting the historic (late 19th century) character of the buildings and the generous landscaping. This reorientation of the building has changed its demeanor from that of an imposing courthouse to a relaxed activity center. Though the new trimmings can be criticized as being too "California contemporary" and somewhat out of character, they have transformed what everyone thought was a white elephant into a center of future development.

street access and better internal circulation. Iron gates were placed at each entrance for security purposes.

Other changes were designed to liven up the courthouse's appearance while continuing this reorientation. A patio was built for an outdoor cafe, using a brick surface, raised wooden planter boxes, wrought iron trellis work and carriage lamp gas lights, and the Cooper House name was painted in gold letters between the first and second floors on both facades. Finally, Walden created a two-story galleria by enclosing a former alley in glass and covering it with salvaged stained glass panels. A mural was painted on the wall facing the galleria, commemorating the original—and still the only—house band. These changes all served to tie the building in with the contemporary, landscaped character of Pacific Avenue.

CONTEXT

From the start, Walden encountered difficulties with local officials, who were unfamiliar with the peculiar problems of preservation. Regulating Cooper House on the criteria for new construction projects, they halted work several times on the basis of building or zoning code violations. The mural was initially forbidden under the existing sign code. Only the commercial success of the project has caused the town to enact

Iron grill and lamps, flower boxes and awning soften the facade.

Looking at the northwest corner of Courthouse Square, with the drive-through facility in the row at right. Continuous cornice line, metal awnings, and decoration over windows create a unified streetscape. From this angle, the drive-through tunnel is not visible.

Drive-Through Bankfront
Helps Stabilize a Downtown

First National Bank   Granbury, Texas

In this small Texas town, the local bank came up with an interesting compromise to solve a common problem: how to accommodate drive-up customers in a downtown setting. By removing a neighboring storefront and keeping the upper floor intact, they preserved much of the architectural character of the streetscape and remained in their downtown location. This in turn contributed to a downtown revitalization; the bank's deposits have quadrupled since 1970 and they now plan to return the drive-through to office space.

The First National Bank occupies three buildings at one corner of Granbury's courthouse square, built around the massive limestone courthouse that dominates the town. The structures on the square are mostly two stories, constructed of brick or the native limestone in a modest Victorian style, and they form a pleasant horizontal backdrop to the eclectic Second Empire style of the courthouse. Nearly all of this district dates from Granbury's heyday in the 1880's and 90's.

In the early 1960's, Granbury was a sleepy collection of historic buildings. They framed the square in an attractive composition: tall glass storefronts, stone arches around windows, and an ornamentation of stamped metal cornices. The construction of the nearby DeCordova Bend Dam, however, spurred development of vacation and retirement homes on the outskirts, doubling the local population. The town's preservation consciousness began to develop in response to this growth.

At this time, the bank was faced with the choice of staying downtown or moving out to a new commercial strip where it would have room for drive-up tellers. "Staying downtown seemed the only right thing to do," recalls Bank president John Luton, Sr. "We were committed to downtown, and felt a sense of continuity with the building. It had been built as our bank back in 1883, and that's all it had ever been."

One problem with the bank's remaining downtown was the inconvenience of the site for automobile cus-

tomers. The bank purchased the adjacent building, a former auto parts store which was now vacant. Without any special design assistance, Luton decided that the best, and least expensive, solution was to remove the first floor storefront and create a drive-up facility right through the building. Rather than demolish the entire building, it sacrificed only the storefront and kept the upper story as storage space for the bank. In this way, the continuous cornice line of the two-story buildings on the western side of the square was preserved.

The only structural work required was the installation of a steel beam across the front of the building to support the upper wall. Luton preserved the original marble tile floor, as it proved durable enough to support the auto traffic, and the stamped metal ceiling was retained. A window cut into the main bank building provided the teller with access to customers.

CONTEXT

First settled in the 1850's as a station against Kiowas and Comanches, Granbury was laid out in a grid pattern with a courthouse square in the center. Its development peaked in the 1890's, when it served as the commercial center for a thriving ranching and farming region. Little changed, except that the buildings settled into decay, until 1968, when a storm damaged the ornate courthouse and demolition was pro-

52

The punched-out facade is less attractive from close up. Nonetheless, the solution keeps the upper story line, and the possibility of restoring the ground floor as office space rewards the flexibility of the approach.

mercial center that caters to local residents as well as visitors because it offers a diversity of neighborhood services and tourist attractions. The bank has grown to the point that it now must expand, and to do so, it plans to reclaim the drive-through facility as office space. It will build a new storefront to enclose the space once more, so that it will again be compatible with the surrounding block. This will be important to the continued attractiveness of Granbury for tourism, as the composition of the courthouse square remains a major appeal of the town.

Putting a hole through a building facade, is, of course, not the ideal preservation solution for an individual structure—but it is better than bulldozing a building into oblivion to obviate what may become a temporary need for parking. Gaps in the streetscape around many bank buildings on main streets across the nation make this solution the exception to the usual course of action. By leaving enough of the building to acknowledge a potential future use, the Granbury National Bank's action in staying downtown helped fulfill that prophecy.

posed. Mrs. A.B. Crawford, owner of the local newspaper, published an opinion survey inviting readers to express their attitudes about preservation. The deluge of favorable responses prompted the County to allocate $73,000 for renovation of the courthouse, to which $185,000 was added in later years.

Two years later, a pair of Dallas architects, Ed Hunt and Bob Reynolds, began promoting preservation of the square. They recognized the special qualities of Granbury and noted that its close proximity to Dallas made it a potential recreation site. Working without pay, they encouraged local residents to support preservation and renovation of their downtown. By 1972, the city council had formed a Town Square Historical Committee to review any design changes in the area.

Today, all of the buildings on the courthouse square are occupied. The bank has been able to sell several of the buildings it had on the market for years, and sales revenues are up. Sales taxes increased from $20,000 in 1970 to $100,000 in 1976; not surprisingly, bank deposits increased 380% in the same period.

The square is now a thriving com-

A Scooped Facade Changes Conservation Policy

Maud Building   Seattle, Washington

The renovation of the Maud Building in Seattle's Pioneer Square Historic District has wrought more changes than first meet the eye. Most noticeably, this project altered the building by hollowing out the facade and creating a recessed entrance. Less apparent, but equally significant, the scheme prompted the city's Historic District Preservation Board to rethink its policy on recessed storefronts. The architect for the project deems the result less than successful and admits that perhaps it never should have been done.

The three-story Maud Building, build in 1889, exemplifies the late nineteenth-century enthusiasm for incorporating exuberant color and pattern into otherwise modest brick buildings. Yellow brick outlines the arched doorway and upper-level windows and forms

geometric patterns in the quoins at the facade's corners. Granite is interspersed decoratively, and floral tiles are set between the second and third story windows. Like many commercial structures of this period, the Maud Building originally had large display windows framed by cast iron columns that extended the height of the first story. It was probably used as a hotel during the Alaska Gold Rush era.

The building has undergone two separate renovations within the past fifteen years. The first project consisted of a general cleaning of the facade from 1968 to 1973. Steam cleaning was followed by sandblasting, a process now known to damage the surface of the bricks. The main entrance to the building was brick paved; inside, the upper-story skylights were restored, the offices were carpeted, and air conditioning and heating were added for a total cost of $200,000. At this time, the upper two stories of the building served as offices and the ground floor as a restaurant and gallery.

By 1976 another restaurant, Juan Miguel's, had moved into the first floor and wanted to convert the basement into a lounge. Restaurant owner Gary Christopherson went to Michael Shreve, a Seattle architect with an office in the Historic District, and the two discussed how to renovate the building in order to allow some natural light into the basement. It was decided to create a light well by removing the glass from the street-level windows, forming a patio or alcove where the display area was, and carving a shaft to extend from this street-level patio down to the basement. Shreve's design called for the paving of this patio area with an exposed aggregate, to match that of the sidewalk, and a curving wooden rail to edge the quarter-circle light well. The alteration also necessitated a new wall and entranceway set back from the street. This new wall was designed to resemble the structure of the facade, with primarily vertical wooden members framing a new set of windows and a pair of doors.

Christopherson presented the ideas and a perspective drawing at a meeting of the Historic District Board, which must approve any renovations within the district. The Board sanctioned the proposal with some specific changes: the paving material to be used was tile, not aggregate, the railing was to be open and of wrought iron, not solid or wood, and the curve of the rail was to be slightly straightened. The Board also asked to see proposals for signs and colors. When these were approved, the renovations were made at a cost of about $23,000.

Five years later, none of the parties was entirely pleased. The renovation has been criticized for both violating the integrity of the building and disrupting the continuity of the street. Gregory Ptucha of the Historic District Board says that soon after Juan Miguel's renovation, the Board made it an unofficial policy not to allow recesses, unless they could be accomplished gracefully and in keeping with the original character of the building. This unwritten rule has more recently been codified as part of the Special Review District Develop-

The Maud Building in 1960, decayed but with original detailing.

ment Regulations, which specify that renovations and new construction must adhere to the lot line. Although not all of the Board members necessarily feel that Juan Miguel's renovation is unsatisfactory, they were concerned about creating a precedent and set down the rule in order to discourage other projects of this sort.

Architect Michael Shreve feels that the basement well succeeds in allowing light into the lower level, and that from the *inside* the building is consequently very attractive. Shreve noted that the increasingly high prices of downtown commercial buildings force owners to utilize as much square footage as possible, including basements, but that often these darker areas do not encourage patrons to venture inside, leaving the businesses unsuccessful. His renovation, on the other hand, created a popular basement lounge. Shreve also notes that the existence of the light well satisfied fire codes that otherwise would have required the addition of an-

other staircase into this small interior.

The architect also said, though, that in retrospect he wished he hadn't scooped out the facade. Part of his dissatisfaction is due to the changes made by the Historic District Board, which he feels did not help the design, and part to the mediocre level of craftsmanship. But details aside, Shreve is no longer so certain that the idea as a whole was well conceived, and agrees that perhaps he and Christopherson should have decided upon a more respectful means of renovation.

Juan Miguel's restaurant has changed hands several times, and successive owners have proposed various alterations to create a facade more to their liking. In 1979, the Historic Board rejected a proposal to arch all of the recessed wall's windows by rounding the corners with plywood and covering these edges with white stucco, perhaps an attempt to create a Spanish/Mexican thematic appearance. The current owners have considered a more

Restoration has brought back the appeal of the polychromatic brickwork, but the ground floor recess has severely altered the building's character.

After a brief heyday during the Alaskan Gold Rush of 1897, the District began to decline as prosperous businesses moved north. The Skid Road, or greased logging skids, left behind in the deteriorating district gave rise to a phrase that still connotes an area of ill-repute, "skid row." It was not until the 1960's that restoration of the district was initiated by a few small developers, whose work prompted others to initiate similar projects. In 1970 the Pioneer Square Historic District was established, and a Historic Preservation Board was appointed to enforce the new guidelines and design review. This legal sanction further convinced property owners that the district was indeed on the road to recovery, and redevelopment projects in Pioneer Square from 1977 to mid-1979 averaged $5.3 million a year.

Seattle has demonstrated more effectively than most cities that a commercial historic district can serve as a catalyst for urban revitalization. The character of older buildings—the quality of materials, the intricacy of their ornament and richness of style, especially in late 19th century buildings—reinforce a human scale and should make them candidates for adaptive use rather than demolition. The radical surgery of the Maud facade, brought about by the very success of adaptive

desirable change: returning the facade to its original hot line. Unfortunately, it is not a matter of just installing new glass between the columns. The basement well, if enclosed, would create an air shaft that violates fire codes, and the expense and amount of work required have thus far been deterrents.

CONTEXT

The Maud Building fronts on the principal street running through the Pioneer Square area. Now an historic district, this was the commercial center where Seattle began in 1852. Prospering from the lumber industry, the city population had grown to 30,000 by 1889, when a fire leveled 25 blocks of the center in one afternoon. Rebuilding began immediately, though, and a new ordinance that forbade wooden structures in the business district is responsible for the sturdy brick and stone structures that remain in Pioneer Square today.

Close-up showing the recess and light well. Entryway is dark and uninviting, disturbing the streetscape rhythm. This drastic alteration caused the Historic District Board to look askance at future requests for recessed entries.

reuse, illustrates the need for more effective design controls. The architect's desire for freedom of design expression has to be balanced against the integrity of the 19th century cityscape or the quality of an individual facade. Slicing out a piece of CFC's warehouse facade might work effectively amidst the drama of new construction in Georgetown's canal district, but disemboweling the Maude Building in a handsome block of Edwardians, while shedding light on the cellar, obscures the quality of the building. As in Edwardian days, some things are better left in the dark.

A New Facade Saves an Old One

Hendley Building (West Section)   Galveston, Texas

The Hendley Building, with the oldest facade on Galveston's Strand, today boasts one exterior wall that is among the City's most contemporary. This new addition is an imaginative solution to two rehabilitation problems: how to save a building with a badly deteriorated exterior wall, and how to bring an older building into compliance with new health and safety codes.

The Hendley Building, constructed between 1855 and 1859, is actually a row of four adjacent buildings with similar facades. The two main facades face 20th Street and the Strand, and total 288 feet in length. With three upper stories of brick, the facade is handsomely punctuated at regular intervals with rectangular granite columns. The corner quoins, window lintels, and cornices are similarly of granite.

This brick row was built, owned and occupied by William Hendley & Co., Galveston's largest shipping company. As the Galveston *Daily News* reported, the Hendley Building enjoyed the distinction of "being not only the first pretentious building to have been built in Galveston, but of being constructed at a greater proportionate cost than any building in the city." The materials used in construction—900 tons of granite, 500 barrels of Rosendale cement, and an untold number of bricks—were all brought to Galveston from Boston by sailing vessels.

During the Civil War, the Hendley Building was at various times used by both Confederate and Union troops for offices and lookouts. Although the Battle of Galveston was fought on land and water all around the building, it survived the war intact, only to be damaged instead in 1866 by a fire from the adjoining building on the west. The fire gutted Hendley's western section, requiring the replacement of heat-cracked granite columns with brick.

A little more than 100 years later, the western end was once again threatened, this time by an owner intent on demolishing the structure, which was now dilapidated. In July 1968 demolition of the section began. After much feverish negotiating, preservationists Dr. and Mrs. John Wallace bought the western section of the Hendley Building, subsequently conveying it to the Galveston Historical Foundation (GHF).

Demolition had already destroyed much of the roof and southwestern corner of the top floor, and GHF raised, through private donations, the $9,000 needed for repairs. Later, the section was put up for sale as part of GHF's revolving fund, but in 1977 the Foundation decided to retain it for a visitors' center and offices. A more extensive rehabilitation was then required. Working with Taft Architects of Houston, in conjunction with Building Conservation Technology as consultants, the GHF drew up plans for a $400,000 restoration project. They raised this money from federal funds, donations from major corporations (including three oil companies), and private contributions.

Plans included the restoration of the original interior partitions and features for GHF's offices on the second floor, and the restoration of the original flag-

The decayed Hendley Building in 1975. West section (at left) was then up for sale as part of GHF's revolving fund.

stone flooring for the ground-floor visitor's center. Most problematic, though, was the west wall. The wall had been exposed to the weather for several years as a result of demolition of the adjacent building, and the weakened brick was pulling away from the rest of the structure. The project engineer recommended that the wall either be completely dismantled and rebuilt or be reinforced by massive steel buttresses. Taft Architects chose the latter option and turned this structural necessity into a functional and aesthetic asset. The steel buttresses became the frame for the new structure, which equals the existing building in height and width (40 by 100 feet) but adds only 5 feet to the facade's frontage. This addition houses the second building exit required by fire code, all lavatories and plumbing, and the mechanical systems for air conditioning and heat. Since these functions are accommodated in the addition, the interior modification of the old Hendley interior was kept to a minimum.

The western wall is contemporary in appearance, in contrast with the nineteenth-century facade it adjoins. Yet the new addition is not incongruous. Taft Architects studied nineteenth-century treatments of side walls, exterior stairways, and use of tile in order to create a modern, yet historically sympathetic, design. The vertical rectangular openings echo the fenestration of the main facade and also create a light and airy feeling; the tiles add pattern and carry the facade's brick color around to the side wall. Together, these features help the large addition to maintain a human scale appropriate to this building and the streetscape.

CONTEXT

In the past decade, more than $4 million has been invested in the renovation of Galveston's Strand, a Victorian wholesale and warehouse district that was severely depressed earlier in this century. (For a more complete discussion of this, see the facade story of the H. M. Trueheart Building.) Today, the entire district is listed on the National Register and once again contributes to the life of the city. While the Hendley Building is but one of the many commercial buildings that have been rehabilitated in this area, it stands out for the imaginative solution to a common structural problem facing preservation architects and for the careful balancing of old and new. In recognition of this, it received an AIA Honor Award in 1981.

A new wall saves a building. Five-foot wide addition contains exit stairway, lavatories and plumbing, mechanical systems, and concrete buttresses for original wall. Though effect is modern, the addition continues the rhythms and proportions of the original facade; the ornamental tile is derived from 19th century styles.

With its ornate carved granite facade, the East Cambridge Savings Bank is a Depression-era gem. Townhouses, not visible in this photo, are to the left.

Bank Gets Mixed Reviews for A Selective Saving of Facades

East Cambridge Savings Bank   Cambridge, Massachusetts

Everyone seems to agree that the new west wing of the East Cambridge Savings Bank is an architectural *tour de force*. Just as the Lord created Eve from Adam's rib, so the bank's architects created a new facade from the richly decorated side of the original edifice. Praise has come from *The Boston Globe* architecture critic, Robert Campbell, the Boston Society of Architects, which bestowed upon the project its Harleston Parker Medal for 1980, and the American Institute of Architects, which gave it an Award for Excellence. The addition is innovative, dramatic, and attractive. The problem lies not to the west of the building but to the east, where currently there is not much of anything at all—and that is precisely the criticism. Until recently there were four buildings on that lot, two of which were Federal townhouses. Despite local opposition, the

bank razed all four to accomodate parking for the expansion. This backstage demolition tends to detract from the obvious success of the architectural show up front.

Designed in 1932, this Depression-era bank building is as ornate as times were bleak. The simple, rectilinear mass of granite blocks gains its distinction from the three tall arches that punctuate the facade and the exceptional carving at the roofline and in the column capitals. Acanthus leaves, half-garbed figures, falcons and griffins recall Byzantine architecture, and their creation undoubtedly served a social function by providing work for unemployed local artisans. Similar carving enriches the arches and moldings of the building's interior.

The structure remained little altered until the Bank decided to almost double the size of their headquarters. The

directors approached Charles G. Hilgenhurst and Associates of Boston, architects, who first considered building an addition reproducing the original granite. The architects discovered, though, that granite was so costly that it would actually be less expensive to dismantle a part of the existing building and re-erect it where they wanted. Warren Schwartz of Hilgenhurst and Associates first thought of removing a slice of the west facade and connecting it to an original building with an unabashedly new glass wall. Both architect and client were aware of the high quality of workmanship of the older building and wanted to preserve it, and so when the firm presented this scheme to the bank directors, they were enthusiastic. "It's what sold us on the architect," said Ralph G. Burstadt, president, and the $500,000 project was approved.

With the help of the original 1932 shop drawings, found in a long-established granite company, the architects prepared a schedule for dismantling the rear of the west wall. Each stone was numbered, removed, cut as required, and installed on the new facade according to drawings prepared by the masonry contractor. The newly-formed granite wall fronts on a curvilinear glass gallery framed with mullions of white steel; this gallery is as sheer as possible in order to emphasize the facade. The new wing, adjoining the old building to the west and almost equalling the original structure in size, maintains the line of the street and even encloses a small garden. The effect, proclaimed critic Robert Campbell, is "delightful," and he noted not unkindly that "the new front seems to have popped out of the old building like a jack-in-the-box on a curving spring."

CONTEXT

The jack-in-the-box is not, however, the only surprising aspect of the Bank's project. It was equally startling that an institution that undertook such a preservation project on one side could simultaneously demolish two historic buildings on the other. These two Federal houses, built in 1829, were among the few survivors of the original development in this area of Cambridge. The bank had owned the entire block for a number of years before applying for a demolition permit to create, at least for the time being, a parking lot.

Hearing of the bank's intent, the

The new addition takes a bay from the side facade and "pops" it out with a curving steel-and-glass corridor. The effect is at once startling and pleasing. (Photo by Steve Rosenthal)

Cambridge Historical Commission stepped in and detained the action for six months while trying to convince the directors of the historical significance of the buildings and also trying to devise a suitable alternative scheme. The Commission proposed creating underground parking, with a desired drive-up window, maintaining the two buildings above and perhaps even raising a new structure around them. Comparative costs were never ascertained, but Charles Sullivan of the Commission estimates that rehabilitating and leasing the two buildings would probably have cost the same as demolition. While bank president Ralph Burstadt claimed that the buildings were in terrible condition, little more than "old shacks," Sullivan maintains they were sound and in fairly good shape.

Nevertheless, the Bank tore down the houses. Sullivan states that the directors "just had their minds set against those buildings," but Robert Campbell is a bit harsher. In his article in *The Boston Globe Magazine* titled "A Conflict of Values in East Cambridge," Campbell cites an imminent waterfront redevelopment project in that area that is already boosting real estate values and will soon gentrify the neighborhood. Campbell postulates that this new constituency would argue for the preservation of the houses, and that the

Bank realized that the longer it waited the more opposition would arise. Furthermore, the Bank has investigated possibilities for a multi-story office building on this site, and it seems clear that the lot may not remain empty for long.

The East Cambridge Savings Bank

is to be congratulated for its prize-winning west wing, but the bank's new reputation as an advocate of building preservation is eroded by the loss of street face to the east. For preservationists, this facade story was only a pyrrhic victory.

The dark side of the bank addition: one of the Federal townhouses demolished for a parking lot.

59

IV · Facades Reinterpreted: *Choosing the Past*

The previous two chapters have illustrated examples of facades restored and facades adapted, with the implicit assumption that designers were working with the original facade. Many downtown facades, however, are the result of accretions of various styles, and this complexity in the streetscape often strengthens the character of a district. The facades in this chapter have returned to another era, but not necessarily to their original form, and often in ways that are startling.

In renovating their handsome facade after a great flood in 1972, the First Bank and Trust of Corning, New York decided not to copy the original after removing the aluminum-and-marlite accretions from the 1940's, choosing instead to evoke the former style with a modern interpretation in oak. Fowle's in Newburyport, Massachusetts cuts a dramatic figure with its *Art Moderne* porcelain facade amidst what John Marquand called a "Federalist Pompeii" of brick streetscape; the renovation architect convinced the owner not to install a pseudo-Colonial front in order to recall another era from the town's past. In the case of Eduardo's in Philadelphia, such a recollection was not even possible, as the existing Victorian facade had deteriorated beyond repair and there was no evidence of the earlier Federal facade. The designer's unusual solution here was to replace it with an orphaned Victorian facade from a demolished building.

Choosing the past becomes even more problematical when a building does not have one. The Oasis Diner in Boulder, Colorado, a transformed 1950's box, dazzles passers-by with its *Art Deco* facade, a style that never existed on this new strip. Cassler's playful facade in Burlington, Vermont

transformed an unassuming white clapboard house into a painted whimsy of the Woodstock generation. Though the building at 400 South Street in Philadelphia had a discernible past, its current owner chose to cloak it with one it never had—a sleek *Art Deco* diner front whose cost he claims were "astronomical" but which he feels was a worthwhile investment.

In all these cases, the new image created by an imaginative reordering or recapturing of the past has been well received by the public. Patrons of Fowle's were nearly possessive about keeping the details of the *Moderne* facade and interior; in Boulder, the Oasis Diner may help to set new design standards for the ubiquitous strip running by it. The Corning Bank has transformed its renovated facade into an image-maker with calendars, cards and renderings.

But there are dangers to a free interpretation of the past as well. Whatever period a facade reconstruction evokes, it must be recognizable within the context of its setting. The Oasis Diner succeeds at taking liberty with the past because it stands in the ahistorical context of the strip; Jim's Steaks accomplishes at the same trick because it is situated on a lively and eclectic street. Fowle's and Cassler's recreate still recognizable periods in their towns' histories, and if the Corning Bank facade attracts praise, it is because the first floor renovation, though contemporary in feeling, nevertheless supports the design of the Edwardian facade. Complexity does serve to enliven the streetscape as long as it keeps within the bounds of historical appropriateness or architectural context.

Historic Town's *Moderne* Facade Poses Timely Questions

Fowle's   Newburyport, Massachusetts

In the restored cohesiveness of Federalist buildings that give Newburyport a special appeal to a surge of new visitors and residents, Fowle's gives the tourist an unexpected encounter with 1940s moderne. In fact, the slick black carrara glass storefront, wide display windows, and overhanging neon sign are not a preservation oversight, but a conscious effort to retain the contrast-

ing evidence of time passing and auto age romance in a downtown dramatically rehabilitated.

The Fowle's business and the building at 17 State Street both have great continuity in Newburyport, but not always in tandem. Fowle's, originally an outlet for Boston newspapers, began elsewhere in 1852. It was only after the Civil War that Stephen Fowle moved

his establishment to nearby 11 State Street and announced that he would:

> keep constantly on hand all the Boston dailies and weeklies, magazines, dime novels, songsters, etc., together with a good assortment of fruit, confectionery, nuts, pastry, etc., etc., and hopes by strict attention to business to merit a share of patronage.

Fowle's did get the patronage, and moved twice more before settling at the present location in 1900. Little is known about the use or appearance of the building before that time. As the business prospered it expanded, and the first floor of the Federal style building underwent a dramatic exterior and interior remodeling under its then owner, Nicholas Arakelian, a newcomer born in Turkey who kept the Fowle's name. Mr. Arakelian wanted the latest fash-

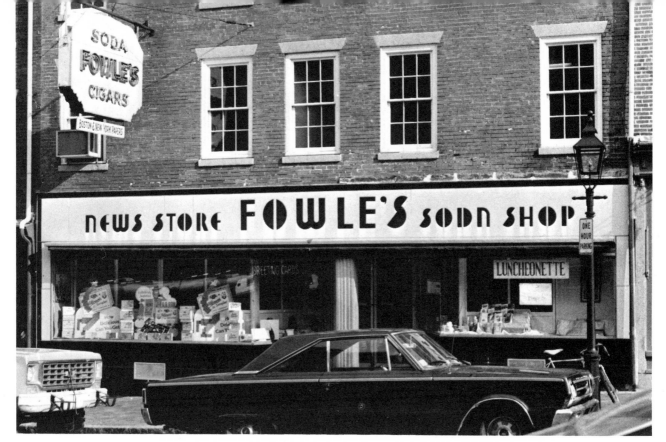

Fowle's Art Moderne facade as it looked in 1942 and as it still looks today after restoration. Sleek lettering, black carrara glass and neon signs are all typical of this style. Decoration contrasts with brick upper stories of Federal-style building.

ion which supported the store slogan "Modern as tomorrow—yet old in the tradition of community service."

From a 1941 mail order catalogue he acquired a complete new storefront in black carrara glass with stainless steel inlay, which opened through swinging doors to an interior of wooden booths and paneling complete with streamlined steel grill and soda fountain with steel bar stools. The distinctive moderne lettering of his large cream and black facade sign was emblazoned across the mellow brick just below the six-over-six windows of an earlier era. A second sign projected from the Federalist brick facades above, and "Greeting Cards" beamed from the large display window, Newburyport's first examples of neon.

In 1955 the present owner, Sam Waterhouse, took over the business and rapidly built Fowle's into one of the largest newsstand operations in New England. Waterhouse diversified into wholesale newspaper delivery service, and added a single-story concrete block addition to the rear of the store to accommodate this business. By 1973, with the carrara glass somewhat worse for wear, and with the facades across the street being transformed with urban renewal funds back to their Fed-

eral appearance, Mr. Waterhouse decided to renovate his store. He envisioned a pseudo-colonial style facade, a popular trend in the 60's and 70's that usually included an out- of-scale broken pediment over the door, used brick on the facade, a vestibule, and multi-mullioned windows stretched to cover the 1940's storefront. He approached Newburyport architect Jonathan Woodman, who favored instead retaining the 1940s appearance. After three years of discussion, Waterhouse eventually agreed, influenced in part by the availability of partial funding from the Massachusetts Historical Commission which would provide support if the "original" art moderne facade was retained, but not for a distorted colonial.

Woodman saw that the store was situated in a block of six connecting buildings which reflected various subtle changes in style from the 1850's onwards. The evidence of these changes included a variety of sash type windows, with granite and sandstone heads, and different gutter and chimney forms. His concept of "commercial archaeology" was to restore the building to its 1940's appearance so that the building would continue the story of change in the block as it was affected by the auto age.

As the work began, there was considerable enthusiasm among local customers who supplied information and opinions on the original detailing of the storefront. Fowle's is a local institution, and local people have feelings of proprietorship. When the stainless steel fountain stools were temporarily removed for reupholstering, a lady irately protested that they could not be removed. "People feel this store belongs more to them than to us," Waterhouse said. Not everyone was pleased about restoring the overhanging neon sign, however, and the Massachusetts Historical Commission refused to fund it. Woodman agrees that it would have been possible to rebuild a Federal front based on analysis of the second story despite the absence of a photograph, but the real issue was whether to destroy an intact original in order to strengthen the aesthetic appeal of a mainly Federalist ensemble rehabilitated or conserved with federal monies. If there had been no original moderne interior, or less reverence for Fowle's as a familiar institution, perhaps the State Historical Commission, which had already restored two other facades on State Street, might have taken a stronger position. The owner paid the $2,600 for the renovation of the large

Purchase Street in Newburyport: amidst a streetscape harking back to the early 1800's, Fowle's recollects the bustling days of the automobile era.

neon sign, which contrasts with a row of new wooden symbol signs across the street.

The greatest problem was finding a substitute for the cracked cream carrara glass panels because the color is no longer available. Woodman experimented with various substitutions including clear glass painted a similar cream color on the back side, but because of the greenish cast of clear glass it was impossible to match the color and it did not retain the same reflective quality as the original. After a prolonged search for a substitute, a colored plastic panel was located to replace the broken front sign panel. The greatest problem with the black carrara glass panels on the bottom at the sidewalk was due to the fact that they chipped, cracked, and scratched easily. After exploring a number of possible materials, it was decided to use heat-strengthened glass that was painted black on the reverse side. These panels stand up well to abuse and can be repaired if necessary by common, off-the-shelf products.

Other work included renewing the soffits and fascia with anodized aluminum, the roof with asphalt shingles, and the window frames and sashes with a coat of paint. Woodman convinced owner Sam Waterhouse not to install a vestibule but rather to keep the swinging double doors. The architect solved difficulties in determining the authentic style, and by settling on natural wood doors with brass diagonal crossbars and fittings in approximate 1940's mode. A square column in the entranceway was originally carrara glass; this glass could not be replaced and laminated plastic was substituted. The old projecting neon sign was taken down and completely rebuilt and repainted, including dabbing on paint to duplicate the original stippled effect. Woodman used nautical hardware to remount the sign, since this hardware was sturdier and improved the sign's swing. The rectangular facade sign was also cleaned and new parts were fabricated and put into place where the old sign had broken.

Woodman was able to employ all local workers, including the company that was originally involved in the installation of the glass front and another company that designed and built the original neon sign. Because of the relatively small dollar amounts of the various specialized sub-trades and the lack of interest of the major subcontractors to act as a general contractor, Woodman chose to have a project manager coordinate and oversee all of the renovation work. Because it was impractical, however, to accept general bids for the work, normal procedural requirements of the Massachusetts Historical Commission had to be somewhat bent, with the result that the $24,200 grant money was delayed for two years while the owner had to pay interest on the construction loan. In retrospect, the architect feels that he would not request federal funds again for this type of job.

CONTEXT

Fowle's is located a few yards from Market Square, the commercial nexus of a city that prospered in the late eighteenth and early nineteenth centuries where shipbuilding, fishing, European and West Indian trade made it a cosmopolitan center. The densely-packed buildings framing the square were completely destroyed when a fire swept the downtown in 1811. The square was quickly rebuilt while a special act of the Massachusetts legislature mandated a new building to be of brick or stone to avoid such a catastrophe in the future. Although the act was repealed in 1832, by then the square had acquired a consistency of materials and a rhythm of cornice and roof lines, chimneys and firewalls which gave it a distinctive integrity as a cityscape. Most of the commercial buildings, including Fowle's stand side-by-side on common bond brick, three stories tall with six-over-six windows with flared granite lintels on the upper levels. A photograph in 1864 showed that broad continuous stone lintels supported by heavy stone rests extended across the entire facade of each storefront. Some of these, includ-

62

ing Fowle's, were replaced with iron beams in the late nineteenth century.

This ensemble survived because the town slumbered after the Jefferson embargo, and despite the relative prosperity of the late 19th century manufacturers, the population did not grow. Much studied in more recent times, as exemplified by the exhaustive *Yankee City* series, it preserved its social as well as architectural identity, though the old downtown had gradually deteriorated, and a new shopping center on the outskirts sapped some downtown business. In 1960 twenty acres in the heart of downtown and across the street from Fowle's were condemned under an urban renewal plan, which sought to turn Market Square into a suburban-style shopping center. The model of this proposal reveals a vast parking lot with a supermarket and gasoline station where a square block of tightly spaced old stores and houses stood.

After the bulldozers cleared 9 acres, the town rallied, and led by some newcomers, sued to halt the demolition and to review the urban renewal plan. They were among the first in the country to successfully change an urban renewal plan so that it recognized historic preservation goals; the remaining buildings in the urban renewal area were gradually rehabilitated, sidewalks paved in brick, and wires put down at a total public cost of $13,390,900. Now community development block grant funds are helping other merchants on the edges of the original urban renewal area. After years of false starts and delays, the largest hole of the original urban renewal plan is about to be mended with a new building. Woodman Associates, the architects of the Fowle's restoration, will again be challenged by questions of time and place that determine whether conformity or continuity prevail in a new facade story. In a city that today largely caters to a new influx of upper-middle class residents and shops, it is reassuring that Fowle's continues to sell newspapers and magazines and serve affordable lunches at its long marble counter and wooden booths. Fowle's asserts that architecturally, as well as sociologically, the town still fits John Marquand's description when he commented some years ago:

> Newburyport is not a museum piece, although it sometimes looks like it. It has some of the most perfect examples of Colonial and Federalist architecture, but it is still a vital, tolerant place.

Eduardo's new facade being dismantled in its old home.

A Peripatetic Facade Squeezes Into Another Storefront

Eduardo's   Philadelphia, Pennsylvania

Eduardo's is a shop in a Federal-period building that wears a Victorian storefront. Eclectic combinations of this sort are fairly common in older American cities, reflecting generations of remodeling. What is unusual is that this particular storefront was originally on a building several miles away and was applied to Eduardo's only recently. This marriage of styles raises a vexing question: to what period should a building that has had a progressively changing appearance be restored?

Eduardo's is located on 2nd Street, a part of the city's old market district known as Head House Square and also a part of the larger area called Society Hill. Although Society Hill had been the heart of fashionable Philadelphia from about 1760 to 1820, it since had markedly declined. Beginning in the 1950's, under the direction of the energetic planning director Edmund Bacon, the city embarked on a comprehensive residential and commercial urban redevelopment program in Society Hill.

The city acquired the buildings in Head House Square through condemnation as part of the Washington Square East Urban Renewal Area. The

Authority sold residential buildings to a number of developers and individuals, including current occupants who wanted to remain in the area and were then eligible for low-interest rehabilitation loans and grants. Several commercial buildings were purchased by Head House Venture, the firm that won a design competition to develop the area. Under the aegis of that firm, Van Arkel and Moss Developers and their architect, Adolf DeRoy Mark, rehabilitated the building that now houses Eduardo's in 1975. Head House Venture still owns the building and leases it to its current tenant.

Eduardo's is a three-story building dating from the early nineteenth century. After deciding that the building was worth preserving, architect Mark was then confronted with the problem that the existing Victorian facade had deteriorated beyond renovation. Mark first considered three obvious options: to reproduce the existing facade, to return the building to its original Federal appearance, or to design a new facade. Of that architectural generation that believes a reproduction, no matter how skillfully done, is at best a sham, Mark

With three feet sliced off to make it fit into its Federal home, Eduardo's new facade seems squeezed and slightly uncomfortable, boldly juxtaposing two periods of history.

CONTEXT

Whereas in the restoration of Fowle's Drug, the architect's choice of historical style came from existing evidence, in this case Adolph DeRoy Mark chose to add on a facade which came from another building, creating a slightly disconcerting mix of Federal and Victorian. His decision reflects an increasingly popular belief that preservation need not mean freezing a building in a moment of time, since the additions that buildings acquire over a span of many years often add character. Mark even tried to create this effect with new construction, in the Head Square Building on the corner of Eduardo's block. This bizarre agglomeration of various Philadelphia styles—what Mark calls "contemporary romanticism"—has been the subject of much debate.

Though Eduardo's is on a much smaller scale, its facade combines the same issues of historical authenticity and appropriateness. In this case, Mark felt that the insufficient evidence of earlier facades justified the rather eclectic choice of another, similar facade. To him, the essential character of the restoration was more important than the specifics of retaining the original facade. In doing so, he has provided a new home for an orphaned storefront.

discarded that possibility. It seemed overly speculative to reconstruct the Federal period facade, as there was no evidence available as to the building's original face, and Mark thought a new facade would appear historically alien. He then recalled that, elsewhere in the city, a Victorian storefront had been dismantled and stored before the barbershop to which it belonged was demolished. The salvaged facade was of the same period as the deteriorated Head Square storefront and looked "quite similar, if slightly less elegant," according to Mark. He decided to attach it to the building on 2nd Street.

Unfortunately, the new facade was somewhat higher than Eduardo's ground floor. The developers, not wishing to mask the second floor windows, directed the removal of a horizontal three-foot-high section from the storefront's center. This alteration disrupts the original proportions and results in a somewhat squashed appearance. But the real attractions of the facade are maintained: its spindled columns, or-nate bracketed cornice and carved appliqué work.

Facade Renovation Plays
Modern Variation on a Romanesque Theme

First Bank and Trust Company   Corning, New York

In 1974, the Corning First Bank and Trust Company rehabilitated its 1903 Romanesque-style facade in modern oak. The renovation, which recollected the original facade design while evoking a contemporary feeling, is an example of the successful modernization of an historic facade.

The four-story cut stone First Bank and Trust Company Building was constructed between 1900 and 1903 as a typical office block with commercial space on the first floor. In 1910 the First Bank and Trust moved into one side of the first floor, eventually expanding to take over the entire building. Between 1940 and 1945 the original pine facade was replaced with an aluminum and red marlite storefront, reflecting the aesthetic prevalent among designers of that period. This facade bore little relation to the building to which it was attached—the lines, the colors, and the materials of the first floor storefront clashed with the 1903 facade.

The Agnes flood of 1972 left the

The bank in 1920: a handsome Romanesque Revival structure with some *palazzo* overtones. The round-arched main entrance faces Market Street on the right.

Corning bank a shambles. The bank had the choice of replacing the aluminum/marlite facade or doing a more historic renovation with the help of preservation specialists. In part because the historic renovation would be cheaper (at $30,000) than replacing the aluminum at ($33,000), but primarily because the bank supported the burgeoning preservation movement in Corning, it decided to restore the facade to respect its original appearance.

Working from old photographs of the building, architect John Milner stripped the 1947 facade and replaced the 1903 one underneath with more resilient materials. In his design, Milner kept the original lines and proportions but he updated the facade with more practical tinted glass and natural finished white oak which replaced the original pine. The new oak facade maintains the lines and proportions of the old facade to present a unified storefront image, but its rectangular leaded windows alter the rhythm established by the upper rounded arches.

CONTEXT

A four-story Romanesque-style building in a block of small Victorian commercial facades, the First Bank and Trust's detailing as well as its height make it a landmark and an anchor on Market Street. As one of the first businesses on the main street to renovate, the First Bank and Trust Company has a large progeny—over fifty of the storefronts on Market Street have now been refurbished. (For a more detailed discussion of facade restoration in Corning, please look at the story on Ecker Drugstore.) Milner's work suggests that one can add modern elements and detailing to a facade restoration if they are done with respect for the old character of the building. The Corning Bank continues to lead the way to visual enhancement of the town center—as its centennial approaches, the bank has commissioned a local artist to create an ink rendering of the structure and has asked Richard Haas, creator of trompe l'oeil murals in New York, Boston, and Galveston, to paint the north wall of the bank by the drive-in tellers. Clearly the bank recognize the benefits of identifying a corporate image with a distinctive building.

The look of the 1940's: red marlite and shiny aluminum, with broad windows. Along with the covering up of the main entry arch, these changes disturb the building's character.

The Market Street facade after the 1974 remodelling. Oak window frames recall the original design but in a modern way. The doorway, though improved, is still flattened, and does not carry on the forms of the upper stories. The wood color is now a dominant feature of the facade.

Art Deco Revives More than Just a Storefront

Jim's Steaks   Philadelphia, Pennsylvania

Jim's Steaks boasts an elaborate Art Deco facade that dates, surprisingly, not to the 1930's but rather to 1976. The facade was the idea of the building's current owner, who believed that the features that made Art Deco such a popular style a half a century ago would still be attractive today. This sleak glass storefront reflects the new life on South Street, the return to fashion of once neglected South Street. The restaurant is housed in a late nineteenth cnetury building in Queens Village, which was last used as a clothing store specializing in top hats. Such finery did not survive the decline of the surrounding neighborhood, and the building was empty when the current owner purchased it in 1975.

Wanting a distinctive look for his first floor restaurant, Abner H. Silver selected the Art Deco style not for historical appropriateness but simply out of personal preference. He employed Philadelphia architect, Arthur Tofani, to execute a design of stainless steel, black carrara glass, geometrically arranged tiles on a curvilinear sweeping facade. The Jim's Steaks logotype over the entrance fits the Art Deco style as do elements in the inside: a geometric patterned relief ceiling, period typography and streamlined look. Good newspaper publicity and the pilgrimages of architectural students add a certain zest, but families and professionals are attracted to Silver's restaurant because it is clean and efficient while still avoiding the prefabricated sterility of a fast food establishment. Silver emphasizes however, that he thinks the expensive renovation is really just "icing on the cake" and believes his location and unique steak sandwiches are more significant.

South Street in 1930. The corner building at left is now Jim's Steaks. Then it housed a men's clothing shop.

400 South Street in 1975, before remodeling.

Art Deco Revival creates a sleek new facade.

CONTEXT

During the 1960's residents successfully fought a plan to obliterate much of Queens Village with a highway connector to the Schuylkill expressway. Queens Village, the poor cousin of fashionable, adjacent Society Hill became a trendy place as artists and craftsmen sparked the neighborhood renaissance. Affluent professionals followed, rennovating town houses in a blue collar neighborhood that kept its noisy vitality. The old movie theatre on South Street now shows vintage films, and a glamorous facade like Jim's Steaks demonstrates that a little creativity can be a great image booster, and that facade rennovations can sometimes take a little liberty with history—particularly where an eclectic population is a vitalizing force.

Deco-Revival Façade Upgrades a Strip

Oasis Diner   Boulder, Colorado

Colorado never really had diners when they were in their heyday in the East, but now Boulder boasts one of the most elaborate examples of "Deco-Revival" architecture in the country. Sited on a busy commercial strip, the Oasis Diner is a complete remodeling of a formerly nondescript restaurant that has set a new standard of design for the area.

The building, a typically uninteresting box of the 1950's, served as a restaurant on busy 28th Street, a six-lane commercial corridor. It was bought by Alan and Tania Schwartz, who had moved to Boulder from New York in 1973 and opened the successful New York Delicatessen in the downtown mall. (The deli has since become famous on national television as the place where "Mork and Mindy" work.) In buying the 28th Street building, the Schwartzes dreamed of creating one of

those "terrific diners" they had known back East, but they had no specific ideas until one night Henry Beer of Communication Arts in Boulder sketched out some ideas on a dinner napkin. "The design was executed almost exactly like the original concept," recalls Beer, at a cost of $300,000.

Beer designed the diner as a combination of newly-fabricated elements and older period pieces collected on shopping forays around the country. Actually larger than most of the original diners, the restaurant seats 200, but the scale of the facade competes well for attention along the road. The exterior is composed of baked enamel panels and horizontal chrome strips, with a broad band of glass ending in semi-circular curves—a form repeated in the doors and on the crest of the cornice. Of course, no diner is complete without its share of neon, and at the Oasis it is

A typical strip diner of the 1950's, with no appeal whatsoever.

used to create a flush sign above the door and to accent the clock which reminds passersby that the diner is always open.

Inside the diner, stools and counters gleam with chrome and booths are streamlined. Coffee urns, cake racks, a clock, and the cash register are glistening objects in full view of patrons. At night, the brightly lit interior becomes a part of the facade through large plate glass windows. The menu is classic diner fare, with malts, sandwiches, and blue plate specials. The first-time visitor finds a dictionary of diner slang on the menu to guide him through his order. The Oasis Diner won first prize in the *Interior Design* 1980 restaurant design awards.

CONTEXT

The Oasis Diner is already a landmark amongst the typical strip clutter of 28th Street. Boulder recently adopted landscaping and sign standards for highway businesses and is planning to renovate the nearby Crossroads Center as a more vital part of the city. Residents expect other building renovations along the strip as a spinoff of the redevelopment project, and the Oasis Diner sets a good standard of design to follow. Building owners need not copy the "Deco-Revival" style, but simply realize that high quality design is just as valid on the strip, where it can create a marketable image that is good for business, as it is in the pedestrian-oriented environment of downtown.

A new style for the strip—not necessarily to be copied, but to be emulated for the quality of its design.

The facade as sign: Cassler's new facade transforms a white clapboard house into a playground of wood and paint.

Restrictive Sign Code Inspires
Facade Creativity

Cassler's Toy Store   Burlington, Vermont

Cassler's Toy Store, set in a residential section of Burlington, Vermont, has a new facade that boldly communicates the activity inside. "WE SELL FUN" proclaims one window sign—and indeed, looking at their exuberant painted facade, one would find it hard to disagree. Cassler's facade is a little bit of the Woodstock generation surviving into the eighties.

Cassler's has occupied its white aluminum-sided house since 1948. Their overhanging candy-cane sign and dancing clowns were familiar and comfortable sights in the neighborhood. In 1976, however, a new zoning setback law prohibited overhanging signs. In response, owner Al Cassler decided to create a new facade for the old store which would incorporate the effect of a colorful sign on the actual building.

Architect John Anderson of Bristol, Vermont applied exposed pine to the old facade and painted a self-designed mural over the entire front of the house: A huge multicolored sunburst edges in under the gable, and building-block letters spell out the name of the store. A curved rainbow, which announces the entrance, is filled in with a black door decorated with the moon and stars.

Anderson also created a 400-square-foot courtyard, extending Cassler's out to the street. Murals are painted on the interior walls of the courtyard, which serves as a display area for Cassler's larger merchandise. Mark Cassler describes his new facade this way:

"Architecture can be a message, a symbol going beyond its own interior use. This building gives something to the street that goes beyond its function as a toy store. It is a 'story'; a story about sun, rainbows, children's play and the liberation of the imagination."

CONTEXT

Located outside the main shopping area of Burlington, Cassler's is in an older neighborhood dominated by big, clapboard houses. Across from the toy store is a bus terminal, which adds little to the aesthetics of the streetscape. The new Cassler's facade does bring life and gaiety; and according to its owners it has been well received both by the neighborhood and by the general public. Business at Cassler's has doubled since the new addition, and out-of-towners travel into Burlington just to see it. The concept of 'facade as sign' can be abused, however, and could undermine the sign code which was the catalyst for Cassler's colorful addition.

69

V · Freestanding Facades:
The Facade as Environmental Art

If a facade cannot adapt itself to changing times and needs, and no one steps in to protect it, the traditional American response has been to pull it down. The Modern Movement, with its dogmatic assertion that a building not lie about its function—that a sleek office tower look like a sleek office tower—could find no place for an elegant old facade on the site even when the building behind was demolished to accomodate the tower. A new attitide has caught on recently in architecture, however—what is rather uncautiously called Post-Modernism—in which an increased concern for appearance as opposed to form has resulted in renewed emphasis on facade design (somtimes at the expense of the rest of the building). Preservationists and community groups may find it easier to save old facades by turning them to new uses, such as park portals or entryways for modern buildings now that it is trendy to see them as *objet d'art*, freestanding sculpture—something to be viewed on its own terms, and not necessarily as part of a building. But as the new eclecticism becomes widespread, it is stirring a considerable architectural debate.

Such controversy surrounds several of the six facades in this chapter. Significantly, all of these projects were completed within the last five years. In one of the first, Restoration Plaza in New York's Bedford-Stuyvesant, architect Arthur Cotton Moore was met with "bemusement" when he proposed saving a typical tenement facade to serve as the gateway to a new shopping and community center for this economically depressed area. While some see the facade as a reminder of abandoned buildings elsewhere in Bed-Stuy, others see it as symbolizing the phoenix-like potential of the community. Developer William Naito in Portland, Oregon, must have met with a more positive response when he decided to save the brick-and-stone facade of the Simon building as a parking lot portal, preserving the streetscape in this historic district of exceptional cast iron facades.

Maintaining the street line is one reason to save an old facade, but often more important are the historic associations that a facade preserves intact. The designers who turned the Mergenthaler Building into loft apartments along old Printer's Row in Chicago recognized this when they saved the outlines of the facade of Tom's Diner as the frame for a mini-park. In ten years, this may be the only reminder of life as it used to be on Printer's Row. Such historic associations were dramatized when the demolition company itself stepped in to save the cast iron ground floor facade of Wing's De-

partment Store in New Bedford, Massachusetts, a 90-year tradition in the city. Wing's facade now serves as the entryway for a downtown park.

When facades stand on their own as portals or "ruins," it is easy to judge the merits of the project; when they are incorporated into larger, modern structures the issue becomes more complicated. In both the Zion Commercial Mercantile Institution (ZCMI) story and the Penn Mutual tower story, some preservationists were not amused or pleased, feeling that the freestanding facades—in the former case, an elaborate cast iron masterpiece, in the latter, a rare Egyptian Revival work—were being swallowed up by the scale of their modern counterparts. Proponents responded that the buildings would have been demolished if a pure preservationist approach had been taken.

Incorporating a freestanding facade into a new structure is less likely to succeed if it is done primarily as a concession to the preservation community without particular regard for the innate qualities of the original design, as appears to be the case with ZCMI. (The institution was threatened by thousands of credit card cancellations when they announced their intention to demolish the cast iron structure.) Another significant criticism of this new approach—one which figured more importantly in the ZCMI case than the Penn Mutual case—is the claim that by demolishing a noteworthy interior designers are destroying the essence of a building. Yet there can be a positive design approach to the incorporation of an old facade, an attempt to create place meaning by creative intermingling of old and new. As architect Charles Moore, noted for the eclecticism of his designs, describes it:

. . . the recent past, the last fifty or sixty years, perhaps quite properly, featured an attempt to clean things up, to disconnect a lot of recollections, memories that in the mind of Le Corbusier and the others of the twenties had grown stale and unhelpful . . . the half century ahead calls for just the opposite action . . . so that those of us who lead lives complicatedly divorced from a single place in which we can find roots, can have, through the channels of our minds and our memories, through the agency of building, something like those roots reestablished.

In this way, perhaps, a freestanding facade is a more poignant element in the streetscape—a tangible reminder of how cities change and what is lost in the process.

Lunch for hungry printers.

Changing times, new uses: condominiums in the Mergenthaler Building, an urban park in Tom's Grill. An unique urban ruin maintains the street line, hides the parking, and recalls a bygone era.

Urban Ruin Pays Homage to a Neighborhood Business

Tom's Grill   Chicago, Illinois

The traces of a neighborhood diner stand as a memorial to the man who once served workers on Printer's Row in Chicago. There are no longer many printers here, and Tom's Grill was forced to change with the times. Instead of demolishing it for parking, however, the architect for the neighboring restoration saved Tom's as a mini-park with its own barbecue grill—recognizing that a Mom and Pop cafe is no longer viable in this gentrified area, but still providing a link with the past.

The idea for an urban ruin of Tom's Grill began when developer William Levy and architect Kenneth Schroeder started to renovate the six-story Mergenthaler Building next door. The ren-

ovation program called for the development of condominium residences on the upper floors, while the first floor was to remain commercial, and Shroeder knew that parking would be needed. At this time—in 1978—Tom retired and closed his grill, providing the opportunity to create the parking space.

Architect Schroeder wished to preserve the main framework of Tom's Grill as a remembrance of the role the business had played in the district's history. Portions of the building were removed, leaving the piers, entablature and ceiling joists, which form a trellis for ivy. The original signs were kept in place along the cornice line, including the classic Coca-Cola buttons that bracket "Tom's Sandwiches." Underneath the

trellis, benches provide seating where customers once lined up on counter stools, and a barbecue allows condominium residents to do their own grilling. Landscaping softens the park and buffers the seating area from city traffic. Parking for the Mergenthaler Building is located to the rear of the park, and residents pass along the edge as they walk to the building.

No structural work was required in creating the frame—only selective demolition. Since the ceiling framing was left in place, the walls had adequate bracing. The entire project, including demolition and landscaping, cost about $10,000.

CONTEXT

Tom's Grill and the Mergenthaler Building are on the northern edge of Printer's Row, an early center for the linotype industry in Chicago. Located six blocks south of downtown, the area is filled with heavy timber and masonry structures dating from the turn of the century to the 1940's. Printer's Row thrived during those years and eateries such as Tom's had a steady supply of customers. As technological changes eliminated the hot-type method of printing, the buildings closed or were converted to cheap warehousing. Tom's Grill, the only freestanding diner in the area, was one of the last holdouts.

Today, new life is coming to Printer's Row, as old print shops are being renovated for housing and new structures fill in vacant lots. Aside from the older brick buildings, there are few traces of what daily life was once like on Printer's Row other than Tom's Grill. The ruin, which received a design award from the Chicago chapter of the AIA, establishes a special identity of place for those who knew the district or live there now. Tom is flattered; he finds it his "biggest recognition ever."

The creators of this urban ruin seem to have saved just enough of the structure to convey its meaning while adapting it to a new use. Resisting strong development pressures on a prime piece of downtown land, they have enhanced the character of the district in an unpretentious manner. Tom's Grill serves its most important purpose not as a park or screen, but as a visual reminder of the dramatic changes which cities undergo.

From Parasols to Pigeons:
Facade Adapts to a Changing Downtown

C.F. Wing — New Bedford, Massachusetts

Like Tom's Grill, the C.F. Wing Department Store is gone, but its cast iron facade remains as a downtown park portal. The preserved facade welcomes pedestrians to a below-street level green area and evokes memories of a company that served the community for ninety years. Surprisingly enough, the Wing facade was saved by the people who were contracted to take it down.

In 1887, the C.F. Wing Company built a four-story building on New Bedford's primary shopping street (appropriately named Purchase Street) to accomodate its expanding business. The ground story was elegantly designed in cast iron manufactured by a local foundry. Though Wing's originally advertised "hoop skirts, real hair switches, sleighs at summer prices, ladies undervests and drawers, parasols and sun umbrellas" among its merchandise, over the years its stock changed to carpeting, furniture, and luxury glassware.

Like department stores in many small cities, Wing's declined with suburban sprawl and the coming of the shopping malls. In 1964, the company announced its closing after ninety years in New Bedford. Public reaction was nostalgic, and the mayor was quoted in the *New Bedford Standard Times* as saying, "Wing's has been a proud name in our family of merchants and there are many who are saddened by the passing of this landmark."

But the landmark had not entirely passed; though the company was gone, the building remained. It was purchased by local real estate developers John C. Demello, Jr., and Isaac Saada, and the new owners there opened a branch of the chain store Korvette's. The store failed, however, only a few years later.

After Korvette's closed, Demello acquired complete ownership of the property and announced his intentions to renovate the building for use as a multi-store arcade. But his plan was halted overnight when, on April 11, 1974, a serious fire gutted the old structure. The City's Building Department certified parts of it as unsafe and authorized the construction firm of D.W. White and Company to take down the dangerous sections of the building. The cost of this partial demolition was $5,000., and the city billed Demello. When Demello declined to pay, a

72

A New Bedford tradition in 1964.

Saved by demolition crews, the Wing facade serves as entrance to a park below street level. A fine work of craftsmanship and a bit of New Bedford history is preserved.

lengthy court battle ensued, and finally the Land Court awarded the Wing Building to the City as a result of tax delinquency. In 1976, D.W. White and Company received a new contract from the City to complete demolition.

It is rare that a demolition crew *saves* a building, but members of D. W. White recognized the significance of the iron work and took it upon themselves to bring it to the attention of the City. Their action caused the City, now more sensitive to preservation issues and further bolstered by an active local preservation group entitled WHALE (the Waterfront Historic Area League), to reassess the situation. The City decided to save the facade, and halted demolition.

Both private and public concerns worked to create the resulting gateway park. Thomas Hauck, an architect for WHALE and a founder of the New Bedford branch of the Friends of Cast Iron, took an early interest in the Wing facade project. Hauck made preliminary drawings of the park and also began scraping and rust-proofing the iron. The City provided assistance in the form of Comprehensive Employment

Training Act (CETA) workers, scaffolding, and supplies. The old paint was chipped off and rust-proof primer and base coat applied before the final coat.

The color scheme of that final coat has proved to be a controversial matter. Hauck chose a two-color scheme, a background of beige/orange with the detail in a rusty red, which he felt was in keeping with the Victorian character of the facade. Hauck and others painted the gateway in these colors, but the City was not enthusiastic about the result. Under the direction of the Planning Department, the members of the Department of Public Works later painted the facade in black. The issue has not been finally resolved; the facade will remain black for now, and when the City further develops the Purchase Street historic park, a different Victorian color scheme may be considered.

Henry J. Bishop and Son, consulting engineers, were hired by the City to work with the Planning Department on the development of this park for the site of the Wing Building. The preserved facade became a gateway leading to a grassy park. The park is L-shaped, extending eastward behind the adjacent

commercial buildings to connect with Union Street. In addition to planting the grass, the City has added benches and encircled the park with a wrought-iron fence made by students in the New Bedford Skill Center. Murals have been painted on the brick faces of the two adjoining buildings.

CONTEXT

Purchase Street became a major shopping street in downtown New Bedford when the demise of the whaling industry in the 1870's led shoppers away from the waterfront area. Today the waterfront area, with its revitalized shops, museums, and new period street-scaping, is once again a popular place for shoppers and tourists alike, while the adjacent downtown area has been less successful. Within the last decade the City designated Purchase Street as a pedestrian mall, but the sprawling North Dartmouth Mall outside the city has still proved more attractive to today's auto-oriented shoppers, despite the plethora of parking lots that mark the urban renewal demolitions of the 1960's.

Nevertheless, the C.F. Wing park has

become a pleasant gathering spot for shoppers and senior citizens, providing a welcome expanse of grass in an urban district. Particularly during the summer, the park serves as a lunch spot for nearby workers, a central meeting ground where senior citizens can feed the pigeons, and a recreation area for frisbee players. Furthermore, with the Wing facade to remind them of the dignity that characterized the streetscape during the last century, several of the merchants are now independently renovating their storefronts. Saltmarsh's, a stationery and gift shop, has redesigned its facade, and the new owners of the Bristol Building adjacent to the park plan to install a Victorian restaurant. The City Planning Department continues to improve the streetscape, and has recently replaced the cement sidewalks with brick and added Victorian-style benches and streetlights. These improvements, it is hoped, will help attract shoppers and tourists who already frequent the waterfront area. The Historic Commission has nominated the downtown area for National Register designation.

Car Park Facade Knits Urban Fabric

Simon Building   Portland, Oregon

Some facades are worth saving not for outstanding architectural qualities, but for their contribution to the streetscape. The Simon Building, while a respectable stone and brick structure with arched windows and terra cotta ornament, lacked the charm and finesse of its cast iron neighbors. Yet buildings such as this, standing in close-knit rows, establish continuity of texture and rhythm and create a distinctive pattern; without them there are only loose threads, not an urban fabric. Fortunately for Portland, the owner of the Simon Building decided that, while demolition was the easier route, the fire-damaged structure could be given a new lease on life with a thoughtful adaptation to a new use.

Joseph Simon, a leader in Portland's turn-of-the century business and political spheres, constructed this building as a luxury hotel in 1892. He embossed his name on the panel that crowns the symmetric facade, and further ornamented the building with iron window grilles, inset tiles, and beaded cornices. The hotel joined other edifices of this size and style in what was then Portland's commercial center.

As the city grew, leading businesses moved out of the older district, which consequently began to decline. By the mid-1960's, the upper two floors of the Simon Building were a flophouse and the ground floor a club for a Chinese Tong. Then, in 1973, a fire severely damaged the building. It was sold soon after to William Naito, a local businessman who already owned a number of structures in this district.

Naito had his reasons for buying older buildings. In an interview in *American Preservation,* he explained:

"I have been in the china importing business for years, and my operations were centered in what was regarded as the 'skid road' side of the city. So, about 15 years ago, we started buying these vacant buildings as they came on the market. We were able to purchase them at their land cost, or slightly below, because they looked like they were ready for demolition."

But, Naito continued, he fell in love with the buildings and decided not to raze but to renovate. Today he owns sixteen renovated buildings, fully leased, and he has a waiting list of people who want to set up businesses in the historic district.

Despite his dedication to rehabilitating Portland's commercial district, Naito thought the Simon was one building he couldn't save. Estimates indicated an excessive amount of time and effort, at a minimum cost of $90,000. Naito decided to demolish the building and use the site as a parking lot for the restaurant next door. Before he did so, his architect, George Sheldon of Sheldon-Eggleston-Reddick Associates, suggested an alternative solution: create a parking lot, but do it in such a way to keep the facade. Naito agreed, and the plan was implemented.

The Simon Building was carefully dismantled, removing the interior and part of the side and rear walls but leaving the facade essentially intact. Sheldon retained the street level posts and lintels of cut stone but, to facilitate the passage of cars, removed all of the window framing members. He then erected a steel support structure as an added brace at a cost of $15,000, filled and paved the new parking surface for $7,000, landscaped the interior, cleaned and patched the facade where necessary, and painted the iron grilles. The total cost of the project, completed in 1974, was $25,000.

The facade serves the desirable functions of maintaining the line of the street and the context established by surrounding buildings, as well as concealing the parking lot. Inside the lot, the plantings and the doorway to the restaurant, with its awning, lights, and shrubs, relieve any sense of starkness and make the enclosed space inviting. The only troublesome aspect of the project is the gaping window openings, which appear rather bleak without their accustomed mullions and glass. Compared to blocks in many cities where demolition has created bleak stretches of asphalt, this is not a serious problem, and the project must be considered a success. The parking lot portal solution, one that should be considered by other cities, received an Award for Design Excellence from the American Institute of Architects and was recognized for innovative preservation by the National Trust for Historic Preservation.

CONTEXT

The Simon Building is part of the old commercial district which developed soon after Portland was settled in the 1840's. These buildings lined the edge of the Wilamette River, and when major fires in 1872 and 1893 destroyed about thirty blocks of the city, new buildings were soon erected. Many of these second-generation structures had facades of cast iron, a material well-suited to the intricate detailing popular at the time and one that produced an unusually handsome commercial district.

As the city continued to grow, though, many of these older structures were torn down, particularly along the riverfront where a highway mowed down one of the finest stands of cast iron facades beyond Broome Street in New York City. Preservation was just beginning to become a concern when, in 1965, a surprise late-night demolition of one more cast iron facade building spurred a constituency into action. Today, Portland has an Historical Landmarks Commission, two historic districts, and numerous historic conservation districts—areas that do not meet historic requirements but are architecturally and historically significant. The City has encouraged preservation by establishing an Urban Conservation Fund, which provides companion loans to private financing for restoration work, and by amending the City zoning code to make preservation a part of the planning process.

City officials are also quick to credit the private sector for funding most of the work in the historic districts. Foremost among these private contributors is William Naito, whose entrepeneurship has produced, as *American Preservation* notes, "some outstanding and memorable innovations for an area that was once known as 'wino town.'" Naito is thinking about adding new construction on the Simon Building that will incorporate the existing architectural relic. As in the Granbury bank facade story, meeting the demands of the automobile age by saving a facade allowed for greater flexibility than demolition would have; and it maintained a human dimension in the streetscape that so often is lacking in new construction designed for the car.

The Simon Building today. Rough-cut sandstone and top floor ornament are particularly striking. Without mullions, window openings are somewhat imposing, but the streetscape is maintained and the parking lot well hidden.

Right: Plantings, brick paving, and period detailing soften the edges of the parking lot.

The facade before restoration: a typical vacant Bed-Stuy tenement.

An Old Facade Measures New Aspirations for Community Development

Restoration Plaza   Brooklyn, New York

Formerly a part of an abandoned, fire-gutted tenement building, this facade now serves as the entranceway to a multi-facility community center, the Restoration Plaza. The center is a focal point for the 330,000 people of the Bedford-Stuyvesant section of Brooklyn, the second largest black community in the country, and an area that for many years suffered from deterioration and neglect. The brick facade serves both as a reminder of the neighborhood in earlier times and as a dramatic foil to the new architecture symbolizing a commitment to community development.

In the early part of this century, Bedford-Stuyvesant was an affluent neighborhood of well-maintained apartments and brownstones. After World War II, the area underwent a dramatic shift in character, as white families left for the suburbs while poorer blacks and Hispanics moved in. By the 1960's, Bed-Stuy was a severely

depressed slum, and residents were disappointed and frustrated.

Riots and violence during that period prompted New York Senator Robert F. Kennedy to look into Bed-Stuy in 1966. He was appalled by the prevailing conditions, but impressed by the many people striving to maintain normal lives. Working with Senator Jacob Javits and Mayor John Lindsay, Kennedy set into motion the legislation leading to the creation of the Bed-Stuy Restoration Corporation, the nation's first non-profit community development corporation.

The Restoration Corporation, one of two Bed-Stuy partner organizations, represents local residents and is responsible for fashioning and implementing community-based programs. Physical development is considered a cornerstone of the Corporation's strategy, acknowledging that the area can never be healthy without a sound and safe environment. The Corporation's physical development program has fo-

cused not only on housing stock but also on community and recreational facilities and retail, office and industrial space. One of their major achievements is the Restoration Plaza Shopping Center behind the old facade.

The Plaza, which opened in October, 1975, is located in the center of the Bed-Study area on a square block bounded by Fulton and Herkimer Streets and Brooklyn and New York Avenues. The Restoration Corporation commissioned Arthur Cotton Moore of Washington, D.C. to transform the site, which included an old milk bottling plant, a theatre, shops, and deteriorated industrial, commercial, and tenement structures. The Plaza today contains a variety of stores, 72,000 square feet of office space, a theatre, an open plaza, and a skating rink. Medical and community organizations also occupy space in the Plaza complex.

The preserved facade is from a typical Bed-Stuy structure, which had tenement housing above ground floor shops. Moore felt that the building with its polychromed brick detailing, stone lintels, and elaborate sheet metal cornices, was not "grand" architecture but visually interesting and worth preserving as a symbol of the street. The initial reaction to Moore's proposal to save the facade was, according to the architect, "bemusement," but eventually the community agreed to his proposal.

As the gateway to Restoration Plaza: banners and a glimpse of activity within suggest a better way for the community.

Implementing the facade project posed some real problems. It would have facilitated Plaza construction if the facade had been dismantled and re-erected, but Moore adamantly opposed this solution. He claimed that, since bricks would break and the mortar would be new, the facade would never look the same. Furthermore, he feared that once it was dismantled there would be little incentive to re-erect the old structure. The project engineer flatly refused to be involved, and finally a consulting engineer was brought in. At a cost of about $60,000, concrete buttresses were poured behind the facade to support it. The fire escapes and signboard fascia were removed, and the cast iron on the ground floor was painted a dark gray. Moore did not, however, clean the brick, as he felt that its aged patina was appropriate and part of the facade's visual appeal.

Moore believes the facade works in several ways. It creates a sense of enclosure while visually still relating the Plaza to the remaining original streetscape. The facade serves as a billboard, since the larger and colorful banners are used as hanging advertisements for the merchants in the complex and announce that something special is within. In a functional role, the facade conceals the new stairways that transport people to the second level of the Plaza. And finally, it is symbolic, a testimony to aspiration hauntingly evoked by the contrast between old and new.

CONTEXT

Some have criticized Restoration Plaza because its empty windows recall gutted buildings in the neighborhood, while others admire the frank illustration of what can be raised from the ruins of the past, that Moore calls "an open gateway to a new tomorrow." Once again, this attitude incorporates a growing belief that a vision of the future is enhanced by an acknowledgement of the past.

Bedford-Stuyvesant has not solved its problems overnight. An ambitious brownstone revitalization program is underway, but unemployment and poverty levels remain staggeringly high. The Restoration Corporation continues to work for Robert Kennedy's dictum that Bed-Stuy is "a place to live, not a place to leave," but people continue to leave.

Restoration Plaza has not been a panacea—but it has been a success.

From inside the plaza, the massive concrete buttresses are visible, as well as the stairways and walkways inside the facade.

Over 600 people are employed there, and community events are held continually. Store tenancy is over 80% (high for the area), and important social organizations have moved in, such as a family health center, a maternity and infant care center, and doctors offices.

According to Ruth Mitchell of the Bedford-Stuyvesant Restoration Corporation, the community has "definitely been revitalized" because of Restoration Plaza. As John Morris Dixon observed in *Progressive Architecture,* the Plaza is "a symbol with power to help convince residents and potential new residents—and the bank they will depend on—that Bed-Stuy has an economic and social future, and is a livable community with the strength—inside it—to bring funds and expertise from many sources to bear on its problems." The incorporation of the old facade lengthens our perspective on this new community development as it records the evidence of what was there before.

Egyptian Revival Facade Keeps Company with Sleek New Corporate Giant

The Pennsylvania Fire Insurance Company
and Penn Mutual   Philadelphia, Pennsylvania

The elegant new Penn Mutual tower, twenty-one stories of dark grey anodized aluminum frames and glass, cantilevers over an old four-story facade, a rare example of Egyptian Revival style in downtown Philadelphia. The juxtaposition of these two structures, an innovative effort at conservation, is the work of architects who wished to synthesize a new design with a memory of the past. Proponents of such a project stand equally distant from two opposed ideological camps: preservationists who wish to save entire buildings, and designers who insist upon the freedom of new designs unencumbered by history.

This facade, although unified in appearance, is actually the result of two periods of construction. As designed by

Independence Hall and the Society Hill area, in an aerial view. The old Pennsylvania Fire Insurance Company building is the white four-story structure across the square and to the left.

the prominent architect John Haviland in 1839, the structure served as a residence and was only three bays wide. The marble facade was distinguished by Egyptoid details: lotus columns on the ground floor and a hawk relief of the Egyptian god Horus above the first floor windows. In 1902 the Pennsylvania Fire Insurance Company bought the building as part of an expansion program to house the Company's headquarters. Theophilus Chandler, the Company's architect, doubled the building by replicating the Haviland facade on the east, and he united the two facades with a marble cornice bearing a hawk relief and the Company's name.

During the following sixty years, the scale of the neighborhood changed substantially as tall buildings were constructed around Independence Square. In 1969, the Pennsylvania Fire Insurance Company Building was bought by its neighbor, the Penn Mutual Life Insurance Company, which urgently needed to expand. The Fire Insurance Company building was the logical place for their proposed new construction.

Because the Haviland/Chandler building was in an historic district situated across from Independence Hall, Penn Mutual was aware that plans for a new office tower necessitating demolition of the Egyptian Revival facade would meet with opposition. Furthermore, the Company was interested in

historic preservation and the possibility of retaining either the building or the facade; Penn Mutual's president, Charles R. Tyson, had served for many years on the board of the Philadelphia

Historical Commission. The designers of the proposed new building, Mitchell/Giurgola Architects, suggested that the historic facade be incorporated into their design for the office tower. Penn Mutual agreed to this plan.

The Haviland facade was dismantled in a process that took three weeks and ultimately cost $130,000. Stone experts Albert Cosenza and Company loosened each 1,000-pound stone from its mortar joints and wrought iron anchors, cleaned its blackened exterior, numbered it, and placed it in guarded storage. Three years later, the dismantled facade was reconstructed at the base of the new office tower, attached to a new concrete frame.

Today the Haviland facade is physically separated from the new tower, standing about twenty-five feet from the building that cantilevers over it from above. The intention of the architects was to re-use the facade as a free-standing sculptural wall, defining a two-level granite-paved entrance plaza. Romaldo Giurgola, one of the firm's partners, describes the facade in visual terms as "a screen; a ruin." The facade, he says, now assumes the character of

The old facade, with its distinctive Egyptian Revival detailing. Most noteworthy are the lotus columns and the cornice decoration.

With the new Penn Mutual tower rising above, the streetscape is preserved at pedestrian eye level, but above there is a dramatic change of scale.

This angle shows the free-standing facade with the entry plaza behind and the tower cantilevered over the fourth story.

a sculpture and a relief, with all of the attendant visual fascination and drama such an object can provide for a public place.

Giurgola notes that one of the major problems for pedestrians along a street of high office buildings is the blank walls and lack of human scale at ground level. The rhythmic articulation of the four-story Haviland facade replaces that void with visual interest and provides measurable human scale. The facade also provides pedestrian orientation, clearly marking the entrance to the office towers a block with some other tall buildings.

CONTEXT

The new Penn Mutual building towers over a predominantly small-scale historic neighborhood known as Society Hill to the east, while to the north a large green separates it from Independence Hall. Because of its historic surroundings, the building has been the subject of some debate among preservationists. English architect Peter Smith, in his recent book *Architecture and the Human Dimension*, writes,

. . . in the sensitive area near Independence Hall, the demands of conservation and those of high finance have come into direct confrontation. The result is the Penn Mutual tower, a standard format skyscraper block which contilevers over the preserved façade of the original occupier of the site. The result has sinister overtones. The eighteenth century (sic) stone elevation stands blind, isolated and emasculated; a dead symbol of a departed civilization. The overhanging tower seems to be gloating over its lifeless victim. This is not conservation. The present has killed the past and left its skeleton unburied.

In response, Mitchell/Giurgola Architects maintain that it was not the entire Fire Insurance Company building that was of historical importance, but rather only the Haviland facade with its Egyptian Revival elements. Romaldo Giurgola states that the re-use of the facade has not preserved a "skeleton" but rather has given Haviland's work a new life, one the facade never would have had if merely preserved as part of a modified structure. Giurgola believes that architects must possess

the ability "to recognize the power of a built structure to become something new in itself," in this case to be viewed both as a valuable object and as an integral part of the new building.

More broadly, Mitchell/Giurgola's philosophy is that buildings do not necessarily warrant preservation just because they are old—at least not preservation in the traditional sense. Buildings that lack architectural or historic distinction need not be preserved in their original form, but rather can be treated in new ways. This view of building conservation, the firm maintains, is also more realistic. It recognizes the economic value of tall buildings in downtown areas, and at the same time allows for streetscape enhancement and makes references to the low scale of adjacent buildings.

Smith's perspective may be determined in part by his residence in a country with a stronger conservation policy, one which frequently specifies the re-use of the shells of older buildings in commercial areas. This approach contrasts with attitudes of architects more firmly entrenched in the

79

Modern Movement, very much in fashion only a few years ago: Philadelphia planner Edmund Bacon recalls an incident in which he suggested that a facade be saved on another building, only to have the architects quickly dismiss the idea as compromising the integrity of their new design. Mitchell/Giurgola's eclectic approach toward a proud old facade conveys a recent attempt by architects to seek a middle ground between these two positions. Despite Smith's epitaph, the Pennsylvania Fire Insurance Company facade is very much alive today, stirring a debate that will continue for years to come.

The cast iron ZCMI facade in 1880, when it had two identical sections and a curved pediment.

Castaway Facade Floats on Concrete Banal

ZCMI Department Store   Salt Lake City, Utah

When the Zion Commercial Mercantile Institution (ZCMI) announced plans to demolish its cast-iron storefront, outspoken residents and an adamant preservation group convinced the firm that the facade should instead be saved. As a result, ZCMI dismantled and re-erected the sizeable facade—in a manner that some find considerably less than ideal. Is this resulting juxtaposition of old and new a suitable display of the historic facade; or is it, as *Main Street* author Carole Rifkind has suggested, an empty gesture to its own past?

The Zion Commercial Mercantile Institution was founded by Brigham Young and other members of the (Mormon) Church of Jesus Christ of Latter-day Saints as a cooperative retail organization. ZCMI opened the doors of the first department store in the West in 1876, and the building was fronted by an ornamental cast-iron facade. Such facades, popular in the mid and late-nineteenth century, were easy to transport and erect since they are actually composed of a multitude of prefabricated pieces bolted together and fastened to a supporting frame. Designed by William H. Folsom and Obed Taylor, the ZCMI facade of Corinthian columns and horizontal dividing elements was probably manufactured somewhere in the East. A local newspaper reported that the facade's appearance had been enhanced by a couple of coats of paint and that "altogether the front is the handsomest of its kind in the city."

This 1876 facade was only the cen-

80

tral section of the current three-bay storefront. As the business grew, ZCMI added on to its original building. A second bay, to the south of the first, was completed in 1880 and its three stories were identical to the earlier ones; a northern bay was added in 1902 after the heyday of cast-iron architecture, and it was constructed instead of sheet tin, although visually it matched the cast iron. The storefront was crowned by a succession of pediments over the years, and the current triangular pediment of sheet metal was erected after the facade assumed its final width.

ZCMI's business flourished, and the department store became the largest in the West. It was so successful, in fact, that the Zion Securities Corporation, the business and real estate arm of the Church, announced in 1971 the construction of a giant new mall to replace the old store. The Corporation planned to demolish the cast-iron facade, citing how little of the early cast iron remained and its unsalvageable condition. As an alternative to preservation, the firm proposed constructing a one-bay replica of the facade, possibly in fiberglass, and mounting it in a niche in front of the new mall.

It was true that all of the facade's ground level columns had been replaced by modern glass display windows, and that the remaining portions were encrusted with layers of paint, but many believed that this landmark was still worth saving. One such group was the Utah Historical Foundation (UHF),

The facade as reconstructed today. A third section, in sheet tin to match the cast iron, was added in 1902, along with the triangular pediment. Restoration has beautifully recreated the original detail.

which had nominated the facade to the National Register in 1969. UHF immediately spoke out against the proposed destruction of Salt Lake City's only cast-iron facade. The group publicized the store-front's National Register nomination and its inclusion in the Historic American Buildings Survey of the 1930's. Members also met several times with a representative of Zion Securities and an architect hired by that firm. Still, corporate officials maintained that there was nothing worth preserving.

UHF member Richard Nibley then initiated an attack on another front. In a letter to the *Salt Lake City Tribune*, Nibley suggested that the only effective recourse to save the facade would be a flood of letters threatening ZCMI charge account cancellations. Letters poured in from all over the state, and many of the irate missives were accompanied by ZCMI credit cards—cut in half. Nibley's technique proved just how strong the preservation constituency was.

Under the increased pressure, ZCMI hired restoration architect Steven T. Baird to re-investigate the possibility of saving or relocating the facade. Baird sandblasted up to fifteen coats of paint off a section of the model, revealing what he calls its "Tinker Toy" bolted construction and convincing officials that it was not only possible to disas-

At work on facade restoration.

From a distance, "postage stamp" character of ZCMI restoration is apparent. The cast iron facade seems out of place and swallowed up by the concrete mass of the new mall.

semble the pieces, but that the facade was unique and well worth restoring. ZCMI directors decided that the estimated $400,000 cost of restoration would be worth the appeasement of public anger, and they announced that the facade would be saved.

Baird initially searched for a technique to remove nearly a century's accumulation of paint. Chemical removers which contain moisture tend to rust the cast iron, while heat removal releases toxic gas. Sandblasting was found to be the only solution, and though it often results in the weakening of the joints, Baird says there was "no damage whatsoever." Having thus exposed the bolts, he was then able to dismantle the facade—numbering and storing each piece.

In order to return the storefront to its 1902 appearance, it was necessary to recreate pieces that were missing or damaged. These pieces included all of the street-level columns removed in modernization and all of the northern bay that had been constructed of the less resilient sheet tin. New castings were modeled after the existing parts, and Baird notes that he was fortunate to locate two of the original street-level columns since these, unlike the upper-level columns, proved to be square. Baird supervised the patternmaking, foundry work, moulding, sanding, assembly, and painting, a process that took two years. By the time the facade

was mounted on its steel supports and standing in front of the new mall, he felt like a self-taught expert in cast iron construction.

CONTEXT

Financially, the ZCMI mall is as successful as the corporation had initially predicted. Located on the site of the old department store and occupying a city block, the mall has succeeded in drawing people back into the downtown area and has revitalized this commercial area. ZCMI has no regrets about saving the facade, which it continues to feature in advertisements to demonstrate corporate interest in the public welfare; even the $400,000 to save the facade is insignificant in a project that cost $150 million.

Aesthetically the project has met mixed reviews. Many Salt Lake City residents are pleased, including the American Institute of Architects, who gave it an Honor Award. Utah Heritage Foundation Director Stephanie Churchill notes that "on the plus side, the handsome facade has been preserved, and its restoration is a marvelous example to the non-believers that it is both feasible and worthwhile to restore old buildings." But she continues:

On the minus side, when viewed as part of the whole Main Street side of the ZCMI mall, it is obvious that the façade was an after-thought in the design process—it has little relationship

to the rest of the structure . . . and appears to be stuck on like a postage stamp.

Others have been equally critical. In *Old and New Architecture*, John P. Conron bemoans the loss of the building's interior, with its soaring spaces and cast iron staircases. He writes, "the heart and soul of the 19th-century ZCMI building is lost forever. Only the empty eyes and open mouth stare blankly from the original face . . ."

Baird did not design the new mall (the architect was Victor Gruen of Los Angeles) and he is not entirely pleased with its appearance, but he maintains that this juxtaposition of old and new was the only realistic solution. Had preservationists been adamant about saving the entire building Baird says, it would have been torn down to make room for the mall. His assessment may well be correct, but Stephanie Churchill's design criticism is still valid. The new mall makes no reference to the facade in scale, color, or material, and the facade does indeed appear to be an afterthought. Perhaps in some instances it is realistic to accept saving face with only a facade—but surely it is equally realistic to expect architects to respect the scale and character of historic facades when incorporating them into modern settings.

VI · Lost Facades: *Illusions and Fragments*

Brendan Gill once said, in his book, *Summer Places,* that "the mercy of memory lies in letting us keep what we have lost." The last rite for a facade can be regeneration on a wall or salvage rights for a preservation group. Preservationists have not realized often enough how artists can aid them in reclaiming the past by recreating, sometimes reinventing it, on a wall. Richard Haas, now well known for his *trompe l'oeil* murals in Boston, New York, and Chicago created two adjacent Victorian facades on a blank wall in Galveston's historic Strand district V commissioned by Historic Galveston Inc. They manage to poke fun at the weighty ornamentation of their cast iron neighbors, and also plug a gap in the streetscape. Terry Schoonhoven's mural in Venice, California performs the same role, carrying the Venetian arches of the building where it is painted onto an adjacent side wall and extending a vista of time past so successfully that it has sparked the imagination of a development team who may replace the mural with the building it depicts. Even when a building does not have an illustrious past, a facade mural can tie it into the history of the surrounding area. On Babel's Paint and Wallpaper Store in Norwood, Mass, architect Dennis Carlone painted a convincing representation of a Victorian storefront on a characterless building and integrated it with the spires and gables of the surrounding neighborhood.

The selective memory of a reliquary, the final bone yard of facades who were cherished too late or fought for

too little, is the subject of the final stories, and they are rather poignant: A brick storefront bay in a parking lot marks Sonora's Chinatown, a redlight district the city council wanted to forget. A little park of marble fragments is all that is left of some of Oklahoma City's principal buildings, torn down less than sixty years after they were built. They were saved by a former mayor, and now are resting in the middle of a parking garage, that probably helped to encourage their demolition. The salvaged walrus frieze on the entrance to the contemporary First California Bank Tower in San Francisco is a more insidious recollection of the past. A token reminder of the ornate facade, which a few years ago, architects did not seriously consider saving, but which in this more eclectic age of Post-Modernism, might have survived, it is now employed as a marketing gimmick by the bank.

The reliquaries, perhaps more so than other facade stories, encourage questions about value. Is it enough that fragments be lifted into the present as reminders of the craft skills of an earlier age? A Japanese can listen to a cricket in his cage and recall the forest now demolished, but is it enough for Oklahoma City to save the cupola of a magnificent Venetian revival building to recall the facade and the associations it holds? Somehow it seems that the selective loss of memory is often greatest in the places which need to recall it the most. But let us begin this chapter on a wittier note with illusions intact.

Street Mural Creates Strand Surprise

Strand Storefront Mural   Galveston, Texas

Amidst the ornate brick and cast iron facades of Galveston's Strand is a trompe l'oeil mural so realistic that pedestrians often feel compelled to walk up and pat its surface so they can make sure it is only a flat wall. This work by Richard Haas, now known for his facade murals in several cities, ties the streetscape together where once two blank facades had disrupted it, while at the same time enlivening the block with a personal interpretation of the surrounding buildings.

The restoration of Galveston's Strand, as documented in the H.M. Trueheart story, began in 1970, but it was never

assured of success. In 1975 the project was still working towards what Peter Brink, the Director of the Historical Foundation, calls "that elusive critical mass" necessary for viability. The architects Venturi & Rauch had just been hired to assist in preparation of a comprehensive plan. In addition, the Foundation had obtained a $35,000 grant from the city to use in marking the nation's Bicentennial.

One nagging problem was the bare blank walls of two 19th century structures in the middle of the Strand, whose facades had been stripped in a 1930's remodelling. This blankness de-

manded attention; Brink says it "devastated the relationships of the rest of the intact block." When he and local preservationist Sally Wallace noticed a news story about a Manhattan mural, "everything fell into place."

The New York mural, a visual extension of a cast-iron Soho facade on its blank side wall, was done by Richard Haas. Haas grew up in Spring Green, Wisconsin, in the shadow of Frank Lloyd Wright's Taliesin East. Though Haas hesitated between a career in architecture or painting before deciding on the latter, his fascination with architectual history—and in particular the American city and its juxtaposition of old and new—remained. Haas was known for a popular series of drypoints he had painted during a 1970 visit— why not commission him to create a trompe l'oeil mural for these two bare Strand facades? Venturi & Rauch were enthusiastic and Haas flew to Texas. He

Before the mural, blank facades interrupt the Victorian streetscape.

Haas' interpretation, with its heavy keystones and exaggerated lintels, unifies the block and comments humorously on it. Shading of decorative elements creates a feeling of dimension.

produced a scale design by studying old photographs of the city, the adjoining Strand facades and other structures by Nicholas J. Clayton, the original builder. The model did not attempt to recreate the original facades but represented Haas' personal synthesis of Strand architecture. In early 1976 local billboard painters transferred the design onto the wall, finishing in time for the Bicentennial Fourth of July.

The mural is painted on a plastered wall with only window openings; it depicts a red and yellow brick double-bayed Victorian facade. Details such as the heavy top cornice, keystones, column capitals and transoms are all outlined in white and meticulously shaded to appear three dimensional. Through its continuation of the style and cornice line of the streetscape, the painted facade carries the rhythms of the adjoining facades, yet—particularly in its strongly rusticated columnature—it adds an individual note. The vividness of the illusion makes this one of the most popular attractions on the Strand.

CONTEXT

In addition to creating continuity and reknitting the Strand streetscape, the mural, as Brink puts it,

> brings a bit of humor to our preservation efforts, which usually seem to be rather serious and intense. With all of our emphasis on authenticity, this blank facade was an opportunity to present an artist's interpretation of the district's architecture and to do this in a way that allowed us to laugh a bit at ourselves.

The artist concurs. As Haas told an *Art in America* interviewer, "Whimsy is an intrinsic by-product of my work."

Whimsy has always served an important function in the streetscape by enlivening the surroundings, by causing viewers to stop and reconsider. Haas' mural continues to provoke animated discussions among visitors who wonder if it is real. It is a solution that other cities should consider to cover the all-too-real holes in their streetscapes.

The Venice of America, a resort fantasyland, seen here in 1906. In Kinney's rather free adaptation of Venetian architecture, the St. Mark's Hotel is in the foreground, the St. Charles Hotel to the right.

Art Imitates Life and Vice Versa

St. Charles Hotel   Venice, California

From fantasy resort in the 1920's, to seedy retirement center, hippie pad, and now trendy artists' haven, Venice, California has often been the home of the surreal, juxtaposing aspiration and reality. Now this southern California beach community, with the dank remnants of its canals, its faded apartments and rehabilitated bungalows, may be bringing back the Ducal facades of its glory days. A few years ago, an artist painted a vast trompe l'oeil mural that extends the arcade of this one surviving palace, creating a vivid alternative to the gap-toothed stretch of parked cars and a drive-in bank. By recalling the plaster splendor of the old arcades, the mural helped spur a host of other street paintings which enliven Venice; now, as the mural begins to crumble, the images it conveys may be brought back to reality.

Abbot Kinney, founder of this so-called Venice of America, erected the St. Charles and adjacent St. Mark Hotels on Windward Avenue in 1905. Like the other original buildings in town, both hotels were loosely adapted from Venetian *palazzi* of the Renaissance. The St. Mark was modeled after the Doge's Palace in Venice, and it was connected to the St. Charles by a replica of the Bridge of Sighs. Both had street level colonnades with narrow windows, grouped together in the center of the facade above; an elaborate beltcourse encircles each hotel, with carved animals and masks at the corners and column capitals. Even if Kinney's interpretations were perhaps more enthusiastic than academic, they nonetheless conveyed the exuberant optimism of early twentieth-century California.

During its first two or three decades, the town of Venice went through periods of cultural aspiration and carnival-like amusement before settling down as a marginally middle-class community. The hotels endured for many years, but as Venice became the gathering spot for Southern California's 1950's beatniks, the buildings fell upon hard times. In an effort to drive the beatniks from the town, officials condemned and demolished the St. Mark Hotel in 1962. The beatniks gave way to the flower children of the 1960's, and the St. Charles continued to lead a colorful, albeit run-down, existence.

By the 1970's, the hotel's facade was depressingly bleak. Over the years the building had lost most of its ornamentation and Gernot Kuehn, in his 1978 *Views of Los Angeles,* published a photograph of the hotel with the caption, "Only the fragments remain of the buildings on Windward, stripped bare, with nothing left to suggest their former glory." But later in that year, the Hotel regained some of its previous prestige. Artist Terry Schoonhoven of Los Angeles thought the broad expanse of the east wall was a perfect site for a mural, and he designed and painted the 52 x 102-foot "St. Charles Painting."

Schoonhoven had previously painted large-scale works, and this $8,500 project was funded in part by a $5,000 grant from the California Arts Council. The design is a mirror image of the facing street with, the artist says, "certain surreal alterations: no cars, people or other signs of life." The mural creates an illusion of depth, as the colonnades of Windward Avenue recede to smaller frame buildings and distant mountains. Overlooking a parking lot, the mural is a welcome addition to the street. Joseph Giovanni wrote in the Los Angeles *Herald Examiner:*

> The mural is no doubt better as a gift to the community than the pseudo-Venetian buildings that once occupied the now vacant lots. One is not really aware that this is 'art'—it is not self-consciously separate and aloof. It plays on its context in very understandable terms.

In its photo-realism, the mural creates a strong sense of potential on the street.

Ironically, this new sense has spawned a rebuilding project which would obscure the mural. Robert Graham, a prominent artist on Windward Avenue, is proposing to raise two new buildings in the original style of Venice, to be used as commercial space, parking, and more studios. These buildings, totalling 55,000 square feet, would fill the empty lot between the St.

The northeast facade of St. Charles Hotel in 1977, a shadow of its former self. The St. Mark's, on the far side of the hotel, was destroyed in 1962.

Charles (where the mural is) and the First Federal Savings, and another lot further down the street. The new construction would maintain the roofline of the hotel and include a colonnade like the original.

Schoonhoven does not oppose the development, since the mural has passed its third year, about the "maximum mileage" for enamel paint in Venice's salt air, and Graham has offered him space for a new mural should the new construction take place. In fact Graham envisions the new buildings as incorporating the work of many local artists for "integral and ornamental components such as the facades, pavements, street furniture and other decorative appurtenances." Giovanni describes the proposal as a style of art in architecture with "a content legible to more than the happy few," and he raises an intriguing thought:

> Were the mural permanent, the wonderful building for Graham to build would be one that mirrored the mural mirroring the old context—a real colonnade coming off the mural's painted colonnade . . . But because the mural will not last, Graham's building would eventually become a mirror without a reflection.

CONTEXT

The St. Charles Hotel and the vanished St. Marks were on the commercial boulevard that entrepreneur Abbot Kinney came closest to completing as part of his dream of turning undeveloped marshland into a West Coast cultural mecca. Using his cigarette fortune, he purchased 160 of the surrounding acres in 1904 and developed an extensive canal system complete with gondolas, a 1,600-foot-long pier with hotel and restaurant, a 3,500-seat auditorium, subdivided house lots, and of course the ornate Venetian hotels. Within a year, he held a grand opening which attracted more than 40,000 people.

Windward and Oceanside Avenues, in particular, had a romantic flavor with their colonnades and mock-Venetian architecture. The 1905 orchestral and dramatic performances in the new auditorium proved less popular than the gondola rides and beer gardens, though, and by 1906 Kinney had installed amusement rides to please the crowds.

The community enjoyed great popularity and success until Kinney's death in 1920; thereafter fire and storms damaged the public facilities, and Venice began to decay. In 1925, Venice

The same facade in 1979, with Schoonhoven's mural. The perspective continues the Windward Avenue colonnade and streetscape into the distance.

St. Charles mural has spurred other street art in Venice.

residents hoped to end their problems by annexing the community to Los Angeles; instead, the city annoyed them by filling in the canals. Other changes followed: oil was discovered offshore, and a plethora of derricks arose; tourism declined; lower property values turned the community into a modest retirement center; beatniks and hippies moved in, attracted by low-cost, deteriorating housing. More recently artists, writers, and film makers have adopted the community, drawn in part by Venice's low rents and uninhibited lifestyle. As Charles Lockwood observed in *Smithsonian,* "People change slowly; places these days—places like Venice, anyway—change overnight."

Schoonhoven's mural, though, and the ideas it has stimulated represent a departure from the manic changeability of Venice, a resurgence of interest in the city's unique character. As a result, many more Venice artists are turning to "place-specific" art that makes reference to Venice's eccentric history—including one mural of the recent disco roller skating fad which has hit the town. Graham says that his proposed development will be "a goofy interpretation of that goofy interpretation" that was Kinney's original Venice. In the swiftly changing landscape of Southern California, Venice's early imagery of palaces by the sea may become in part a reality once more as the past repeats itself.

A Trompe L'Oeil Past Embellishes A Building Without One

Babel's Paint & Wallpaper   Norwood, Massachusetts

As some of the stories here reveal, improving a facade by restoring it to an earlier appearance is sometimes costly or impractical, but in the case of this Norwood, Massachusetts building it was not even possible. Constructed in 1963, the building embodied the worst aspects of commercial architecture of that period: an uncompromising rectilinearity and starkness, with only a sign to indicate its identity. Although the building had served several functions—grocery store, furniture warehouse, doughnut factory, and catering business—none had made any lasting impression upon the facade. This concrete box simply had no past worth recalling, and new owner Victor Babel, Jr., was faced with the problem of creating an identity for an existing but undistinguished building.

Babel, who bought the building to serve as the new home for the 30-year-old-paint and wallpaper business he inherited from his father, was inspired by a popular building improvement project in Boston: Richard Haas' architecturally-derived mural that enlivens the rear wall of the Boston Architectural Center. Babel saw no reason why such projects should be confined to the city, and, appropriately, he "wanted to show people what they can do with paint." He settled on the idea of a facade mural and contacted artist George Vogt and architect Dennis Carlone for design assistance.

Dennis Carlone suggested they create a realistic mural with historic references. Babel's building was undeniably bland and contemporary, but Carlone discovered it was near Norwood's Gothic Revival town hall and two churches of that same style. Neighboring houses also date from the nineteenth century, and Carlone thought that Babel's mural should acknowledge that period. Accordingly, the mural transforms a side wall of the former warehouse into a two-story shop in an approximate late-nineteenth century mode.

Carlone articulated the long expanse of the facade into several segments, with painted display windows divided by vertical members resembling cast iron columns. The clerestory window appropriately capped by a horizontal lintel, serves as a sign area and also divides the facade convincingly into two stories. Rounded windows in the upper story are embellished with sills and peaked bargeboards, shadowed in black. Although most of the facade design is as imaginary as it is referential, the pattern used in the roofline cornice is derived from the bell tower of nearby St. Catherine's Church.

The mural was executed during the summer of 1979 and cost approximately $8,000, financed privately. Wall surfaces were steamed and prepared, a process that took about three weeks, and George Vogt was assisted by Vic Babel in the five weeks of painting that followed. They painted the mural with regular Latex house paint, using mostly standard colors, while shaded colors were mixed on Babel's own machines. Although only the facade is detailed, the other three walls are painted brick red to match the upper story of the facade. As Dennis Carlone notes, this treatment of the four sides is "much like a true building of the times."

Babel's utilizes two types of sign: lettering on the illusionistic windows, which resembles stencilling common to that period, and a long, carved name sign. This latter—real—sign was made by Bob Dias of Norwood for Babel's former store, and cost $450 in 1975. Another notable feature of the project is the pair of sequoia wood doors made by cabinetmaker Dennis Bradford. Bradford had designed doors for another Victorian restoration, and that design was slightly modified for Babel's. Including installation, the elegant doors cost $2,000, bringing the total project cost to approximately $10,450.

CONTEXT

Babel's mural has been well received. Vic Babel says that people who are just driving by stop in to compliment him, and he has been honored at a Chicago trade convention as well as by the Chamber of Commerce and the Norwood Selectmen. As the Chamber of Commerce observed, Babel's effort not only enhances the neighborhood but also benefits all of Norwood. "I wanted to do it because I have pride in the town," said Babel, and evidently his project has inspired similar sentiment in others. Within a year of the project's completion, many of the nearby homeowners had independently painted their houses. Town maintenance of the public parking lot that adjoins Babel's has dramatically improved, and vandalism of the mural, which many Norwood residents had feared, hasn't happened. "The police feel they have to protect it," Babel commented, noting that the police now check on the building more often than they did before. This increased protection is certainly a crime deterrent but, as Babel also observed, many murals in Boston and other large cities are similarly undisturbed by graffiti, even where police patrols are lacking. Perhaps even vandals, whose main motive is often to achieve some recognition in a world that particularly threatens them with anonymity, can respect the special efforts that others make to dignify a place, even when they are illusionary.

A common sight in American cities.

A convincing Victorian fantasy in red with period lettering. The gables echo nineteenth century rooflines to the left.

Happy Pen Chow, one of Sonora Chinatown's last residents. He died before this, the last building in the district, was razed.

Facade Epitaph to a Past City Fathers Would Just as Soon Forget

Chinatown Marker   Sonora, California

All that remains of Sonora's once-bustling Chinatown is a single brick bay of a building facade in the middle of a downtown parking lot. Constructed from materials retrieved during the demolition of Chinatown's last structures, the brick marker is a cenotaph to what Sonora's council cared not to remember—the red light district.

Sonora is a small town nestled in the foothills of the Sierras; the population is 3,600. But in the 1850's, as one of the many California towns settled during the Gold Rush, Sonora had a population of over 20,000. First Mexican, and then Chinese immigrants clustered in this section of the town, behind the main business district, in tightly packed brick and wooden one-story structures. Over the years, as the Chinese inhabitants gradually died out, the wooden buildings deteriorated and were pulled down. Finally, the only remnants of Sonora's Chinatown were

two badly dilapidated brick structures on the edge of a downtown parking lot. In 1970, the City of Sonora bought the property, intending to raze the buildings for more parking spaces.

But members of the Sonora-based Tuolumne County Historical Society (TCHS) came to a city council meeting, plans for the restoration and re-use of one of the buildings tucked under their arms. Arguing for the preservation of Sonora's only remaining Chinatown structures, the TCHS proposed spending $17,555 to reinforce one of the building's facades, tear out the roof and side wall, and create a mini-park behind, not unlike the Wing facade park in New Bedford. The TCHS requested $4,900 from the city, saying that the remaining $12,655 would be raised through private donations and raffles.

The five-man city council rejected the proposal. Although they had

$86,000 in uncommitted money in their general fund, and $207,000 in matured deposits, the city did not, they maintained, have the $4,900 to help the TCHS save the buildings. The TCHS protested the decision, and the city council delayed further action until the next budget meeting.

In the meantime, community sentiment both for and against the building grew. Some, such as Superior Court Judge Ross Carkeet, remembered the buildings fondly:

On nearing this building one could hear the Chinese gambling with Chinese checkers and playing Fan Tan. They raised quite a din with their voices, but one thing was certain—that during the games each gambler had a dish of rice and a cup of hot tea at his elbow.

City Planning Commission member Ros Green remembered the buildings in a considerably different light. "Knock down those horrible old buildings," Green said at one meeting, describing them as a "fifth-rate cat house," where "the miners went upstairs to get hot pants," Merle Crandall, a Sonora citizen, was horrified at the TCHS's attempt to save the buildings. "What kind of people are these," he asked in the local paper, "that want to honor a house of prostitution?"

On April 11, 1971, the city council had its regular meeting. The question of the two buildings' destruction was not on the published agenda, and the TCHS was not invited to attend the meeting. Although the council had promised to reconsider the preservation of the buildings at the subsequent budget meeting, council members chose that night to vote for the buildings' destruction, 4–1. The demolition was scheduled for April 13, 1971—two days after the vote was taken.

At 5:30 a.m., before most people had risen for the day, a backhoe tugged at the last historic facade of Chinatown, and the bricks spilled out into the adjoining street. When Alvin Sylva of the TCHS found out that the razing had already begun, he rushed over with his pickup truck and salvaged three loads of bricks and two iron shutters from the ruins.

Disappointed at the city's behavior, but determined to commemorate Sonora's Chinatown somehow, the TCHS raised money from a raffle in order to build a monument from the salvaged bricks. The marker, which was erected

This memorial is the only hint the youngsters at right will have of Sonora's Chinese heritage.

in 1974 by Mason Inslee Rude, is a walk-in structure in the style of an old brick facade flanked by two original iron shutters. Inside on the back wall a plaque is mounted recalling the history of old Chinatown.

CONTEXT

The crumbling brick structures of Sonora's Chinatown may not have been beautiful or architecturally significant, even in the minds of the most ardent preservationist, but they nonetheless served as a visible reminder of the town's heritage. In the Tom's Grill facade story, an "urban ruin" of a modest storefront was retained along changing Printer's Row of Chicago because it provided a link with past identity, no matter how commonplace—an example of new attitudes toward preservation. Here in Sonora a few years earlier, the town fathers clearly wanted to forget Chinatown and the remnants of the town's not-so-prim heritage, though the Gold Rush imagery remains a marketing ploy to attract tourists to Main Street. This type of selective memory can foreshorten today's perspective; indeed, the councilmen could not see beyond the need for six additional parking spaces. The spectacle of shiny cars nudging the rebuilt brick facade bay has a surreal poignance for those who still carry memories associated with the real Sonora Chinatown.

Mini Reliquary in a Garage Commemorates a City's Lost Face

Clarence Ford Park   Oklahoma City, Oklahoma

Named after a prominent city businessman, Clarence Ford Park sits in the central well of the Santa Fe Plaza parking garage in downtown Oklahoma City. Resting within it are the relics saved from some of the dozens of buildings felled in one of the most massive urban renewal projects in the country. In fact, more of old Oklahoma City may be in the park as decapitated ruins than out on the streets, where nearly everything was bulldozed into oblivion.

After a prolonged post-war period of urban flight, Oklahoma City was one of the first cities to embrace the urban renewal panacea. The internationally known firm of I.M. Pei drew up a plan in 1964 that called for the destruction of much of the downtown and a massive rebuilding effort. Like many another city, Oklahoma City was to dynamite its existing buildings and replace them with the glittering functionalist boxes that the sixties loved.

Little opposition arose, and at the ripe age of 75, Oklahoma City began the systematic destruction of its downtown.

One who felt somewhat ambivalent about the destruction was former mayor George Shirk, who tried unsuccessfully to conserve some of the more beautiful buildings. Such plans were always refused for financial reasons. Unable to stem the tide of destruction, Shirk began to collect decorative elements from the buildings as they were leveled. He donated them to the Chamber of Commerce with the intention of exhibiting them in a public space.

In 1969, the city was finishing construction on Santa Fe Plaza, a six-story parking garage built on the former site of several brick warehouses. The building had been financed by the sale of revenue bonds, and was to include office space on the ground level. The Chamber of Commerce, as an underwriting agent for the bond sale, agreed

to move its operations into the Plaza. An open well in the middle of the complex, immediately adjacent to the Chamber offices, seemed like a good location for the mini-park exhibiting what was left of Oklahoma City's past.

Arranged on pedestals at the entrance to the 25′ x 50′ landscaped park are three finials from the Criterion Theatre, once an elaborate movie palace decorated in terra cotta. A cupola from the Baum Building, designed in 1910 by Sol Layton and based on the Doge's Palace in Venice, is identified with a plaque that calls it "one of Oklahoma City's most beautiful buildings." Another Layton work of 1910, the Patterson Building, is represented by an ornate rooftop light fixture which has been converted to a fern planter. The park also includes four cast iron benches from the old Santa Fe Railroad Terminal, a fountain, and a few tables.

Since the park is not visible from the street and is not advertised, few local

Oklahoma City before urban renewal. Most of these buildings are now gone.

The Baum Building, modeled after the Doge's Palace in Venice. It was built in 1910 and razed less than sixty years later.

All that remains of the Baum Building: a cupola in Clarence Ford Park.

residents seem to be aware of it. Many of the people who work in the Santa Fe complex, however, have discovered the park as a pleasant lunchtime spot. The Chamber of Commerce considers it a success.

CONTEXT

"Urban renewal was the same here as anywhere else," says Sandy Stratton of the Oklahoma State Historic Preservation Office. "We were just very slow in organizing to stop it." There was no preservation movement ten years ago, and public consciousness of the issue has grown only in the last five years. Today the bulldozing has just about stopped, with a handful of old buildings saved by historic register certification, thanks to the diligent efforts of a few individuals. These buildings are now being restored.

But the general attitude toward urban renewal remains the same. A 1980 Chamber of Commerce publication proclaimed:

> Most of what needed to be torn down—such as the Hales Building and the Biltmore Hotel—have long been dynamited and bulldozed into history, occasionally over the howls of some groups. In some cases, the holes left behind were ugly, but not nearly as ugly as the crumbling, outdated buildings which were razed. Fortunately, the holes are proving only temporary. They are being methodically replaced with gleaming office towers and modern public facilities befitting one of the nation's most vibrant and prosperous communities.

In the race to build the functional, characterless city, Oklahoma City seems to have moved with amazing speed, obliterating many of its finest structures when they were barely 50 years old.

For Oklahoma citizens interested in their heritage, it is a saddening and embarrassing situation. "The city was practically leveled," says Stratton. "We lost some gorgeous things." She recounted an incident where an AIA task force on historic structures visited Oklahoma City, and the preservation office didn't know where to take them for a tour. It is one of those places that, in the words of Gertrude Stein, has "no there, there." To see what is left of the former Oklahoma City, one must wander into a tiny courtyard in the middle of a parking garage.

The Alaska Commercial Building. A profusion of ornament: Corinthian columns, walruses, bear heads, wreaths. The building is scaled to function and treated as a column, its tripartite sections divided by horizontal bands of decoration.

Facade Walruses: Off the Ledge and Into the Advertisements

California First Bank   San Francisco, California

The severe facade of the new California First Bank incorporates a few decorative relics from its predecessor on the site, the Alaska Commercial Building. The headquarters of an important firm in the development of commerce in the North Pacific, it was an elegant structure that celebrated its activity with a wealth of unique carved stone ornamentation. Today the remaining fragments, a small portion of the old building's grandeur, are stuck onto the

93

new facade as a token nod to the past, with an emptiness of feeling that makes the destruction of this monument somehow more contemptible.

The Alaska Commercial Company, founded in 1868, held exclusive rights to the taking of fur seals in parts of Alaska for more than a decade; they also played a part in the Yukon Gold Rush. Originally located in a four-story building at the corner of Sansome and California Streets, the company decided to erect a new building on this same site shortly after the 1906 earthquake.

Designed by Henry H. Meyer and Clarence Ward, the new building was a rectilinear eleven-story tower with a dramatic entrance marked by Corinthian columns. The structure itself was divided like a column into three exterior sections. The tripartite design corresponded to the building's functions: entrance and shops at the base, offices in the middle shaft, and mechanical equipment in the capital at the top. The building's particular appeal, however, was its ornamentation. Tusked walruses, polar bears, fish, seals, sea monsters, icicles, and rope, all carved from granite, served to "delight the imagi-

nation and evoke a sense of San Francisco's more romantic and adventurous past," as the city's historic preservation organization, San Francisco Heritage, later proclaimed. The ornaments surrounded the building on protruding cornices, easily visible from the street. The detailing in the building's interior was equally ornate, especially in the lobby with its marble, delicate gilded iron, and sea shell lamps.

The building served as the headquarters of the Alaska Commercial Company until 1940 and subsequently housed a variety of offices. In December of 1972, the San Francisco Examiner and Chronicle announced that "the highest known price for land in California history was recorded last week," as the Bank of Tokyo paid $2.5 million for the Alaska Commercial Building. They determined to construct their new California First Bank headquarters on the site, and announced their intention to demolish the ACB.

Preservationists were understandably unhappy about the decision to demolish the building. In *Here Today,* the city-wide architectural survey adopted by the Landmark Board, Planning

Commission, and Board of Supervisors, the ACB was reviewed by nine professional consultants and received high praises for both architectural and historical significance. The City's Landmark Preservation Advisory Board, with limited powers, discussed the possibility of designating the ACB as a landmark, but concluded that it was already too late for such action. The Board instead wrote to the Bank and requested that it consider retaining the building, as did the National Trust for Historic Preservation.

But the Bank was not to be deterred. In a letter to the president of the National Trust, project manager Howard A. Leif agreed that the exterior of the ACB had "some interesting features" but said that it would not be feasible to preserve the facade. Leif defended the demolition on two grounds: first,

> "the extremely high price paid for this property dictates that it must be replaced by a functional and more productive structure;"

and second,

> "the very elements (extruding stone figures, overhanging cornices, etc.)

All that remains: a walrus frieze grafted onto "a functional and more productive structure"—merely a token gesture.

"You've come a long way, walrus"??

which make the existing building interesting are in themselves a real danger to pedestrian life in the event of a severe earthquake."

Heritage met with the project architects and the Bank officers and made specific recommendations as to how the ACB could be saved and why, in fact, costs could be thus reduced—to no avail. The ACB suffered a final blow in the Environmental Impact Report prepared by the City Planning Commission. The Planning Commission simply reiterated the conclusions of the Bank's development consultants; alternatives to demolition were not seriously considered. The report concurred that it would be "excessively costly" to bring the building up to present fire and seismic safety code standards; that the Bank could not build elsewhere as this was "the only available site in the core of the financial district of the appropriate size;" and that the Bank could not remain at its current site because of overcrowding and a vague threat of lease expiration. Clearly, the new construction was sanctioned by the City, and when Heritage appealed the issuance of the demolition permit before the Permit Appeals Board, the Board denied their request. The Alaska Commercial Building was demolished in 1975.

The Bank's architects, Skidmore, Owings, and Merrill, erected a 22-story structure on the site. They did, however, salvage a frieze of the old granite walruses which they placed near the entrance of the new Bank and at the rear—"a place of honor on the same site," as the Bank's advertisement states. The walrus frieze hangs against a blank wall at a right angle to the entry. The bank continues to use the walrus as an advertising symbol; plastic walrus-head piggy banks were giveaways to new customers, and in one advertisement the copy concluded with the slogan, "You've come a long way, walrus."

CONTEXT

The case of the California First Bank raises the issue of preservation economics. Across the country, older buildings occupy many acres of prime commercial real estate in our cities. From a purely economic standpoint, these older buildings do not make optimum use of their sites. This argument has often served as justification for demolition, and so long as government tax policy rewarded new construction rather than adaptive use, and local zoning does not restrict zoning envelopes, the demolition continued. The California First Bank paid an enor-

mous sum for their site, and they had nothing to lose financially by tearing down the ACB, because preservation incentives were not strong enough to withstand the economic gains of higher zoning density, and the current tax credits for adaptive use were not then available.

There are proven alternatives to demolition: in San Francisco alone, two other banks (the Bank of California and Citizens Savings) have incorporated older existing buildings into their new construction, and the results are laudable. But more recently, the California Supreme Court denied a preservation plea and approved the demolition of San Francisco's elegant City of Paris building. Neiman-Marcus is erecting a new five-story department store on the site, stating among other reasons that the cost of earthquake-proofing made rehabilitation of the existing structure "infeasible," and that the floor plan could not accomodate the necessary alterations for shopping. When preservation interests are pitted against economic advantage, many corporations still unhesitatingly choose the latter, as the tokenism of plastic walrus banks attests.

This row of storefronts in Buena Vista, Colorado, presents a classic lesson in what can go wrong when people try to improve their business image without considering the value of their original facades.

Appendix
How to Improve Your Facade:

Some Guidance for Main Street Merchants and Their Designers

with Noré V. Winter

Many of the facade stories in previous chapters of this book have discussed major transformations: facades taken down and reassembled, storefronts turned into park portals, old facades tacked onto new buildings, and new facades laminated to old buildings. Such radical alterations are not required, and cannot be afforded by many merchants in the Main Street districts of American cities and towns. Usually, these merchants and property owners will not be turning dry goods buildings into an architectural *tour de force* like Louisville's new natural history museum, but rather they simply want to invest a small amount of money to make their stores attractive enough to improve sales. This chapter addresses these renovations of a modest sort, and gives advice regarding changes that are both needed and affordable for Main Street facades.

The nineteenth-century banks, pharmacies, and clothing stores that line Main Streets across the country have typically changed appearance over the years not once but several times. These alterations are as predictable as they are numerous: a paint job and a new plastic sign covering earlier lettering, the boarding up of old window openings and the creation of wide new show windows, the replacement of a carved wooden door by one of a glass and aluminum, and the covering of a detailed brick front with metallic panels. All too often, the changes have been unsympathetic to the original character of the building and to the street. A glance at most Main Streets reveals a cacophony of first story renovations in sleek artificial materials, rough field stone, colonial brick, or board and batten. In contrast to the collected ordering of architectural elements on the upper floors, they have the same effect as bright polyester trousers at a dinner party in formal dress.

Fortunately, merchants, bankers, property owners, and architects in increasing numbers are coming to realize the value of rehabilitation schemes that reveal, rather than conceal, the architectural qualities of existing facades. This appendix examines facades within the context of Main Street design. It reviews the patchup and new image approaches in order to demonstrate the need for a simpler enhancement method that respects the character of the existing streetscapes across America. It then discusses some of the key components affecting facade renovation—signs, paint, ornament, cleaning, and financing. Finally, it describes six storefront renovations which demonstrate how some of the suggestions regarding these components have been applied.

Although the specific techniques vary, the projects share common concerns. Each acknowledges that budget constraints on Main Street must be faced realistically. These projects are low cost: some schemes are little more than a fresh coat of paint or removal of previous "improvements." Each rehabilitation respects the integrity of the building front. The facade commands attention not through oversized signage or garish color combinations but by defining a coordinated, unified image. Although each project supports the building's traditional appearance, the intent is not to create preservation show pieces. These are not historically-accurate "restorations" but rather practical "rehabilitations." Modern materials are often used, sometimes to simulate older, more expensive materials, and the building accommodates current needs even if it must be accordingly altered from its original appearance. Though these facade renovations are not large in scale, the results are often surprisingly dramatic.

FACADE TREATMENTS

Why Merchants Renovate Facades

Renovation is frequently chosen as the solution to visual, structural, and financial problems. Visual or cosmetic renovations, which serve as a sort of streetside advertising, are undertaken by both established and fledgling businesses. A merchant who has occupied the same shop for a long period of time may renovate because of a wish to upgrade or update his image. Alternatively, a merchant moving into a new location may want to make his presence widely known. Both sorts of renovations are done in the hope of stimulating business.

The most common cause of a renovation for structural reasons is a change of location. If a tenant is moving into a building and intending to use it for a new, significantly different use, then structural considerations may make him decide to renovate both inside and out. And, in the case of buildings that are leased rather than owner-occupied, the landlord often initiates a renovation or approves his tenant's renovation plans since the work done will improve the value of the property and can serve as the basis for a rent increase.

These reasons for renovation are not all equally valid, and perhaps one key to inspiring good renovations is to make sure that they are done for the right reasons. The continual struggle to update a shop's image usually results in a "keeping up with the Jones'" type of accumulation. Each sign attempts to be larger than the last and sometimes bigger than every other on the street, and the new quickly becomes the old size or color that must be surpassed. This type of alteration wastes money, erodes the character of a streetscape, and usually does not even achieve its goal of being unique.

Renovation should be seen as one

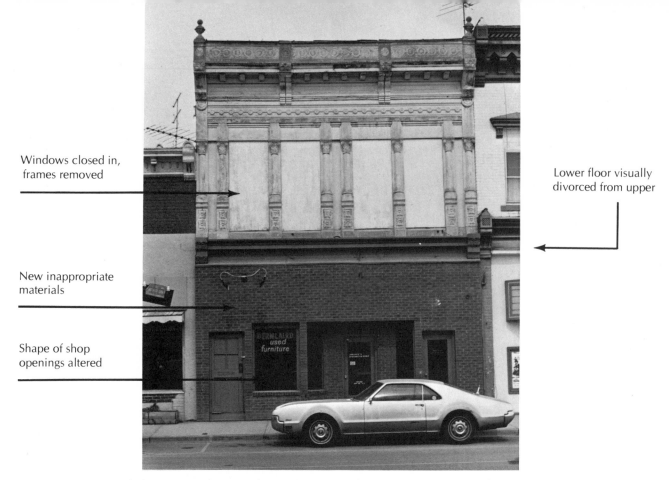

Windows closed in, frames removed

New inappropriate materials

Shape of shop openings altered

Lower floor visually divorced from upper

Blocking up second story windows and "modernizing" first floor shops are typical alterations that weaken the visual impact of this facade.

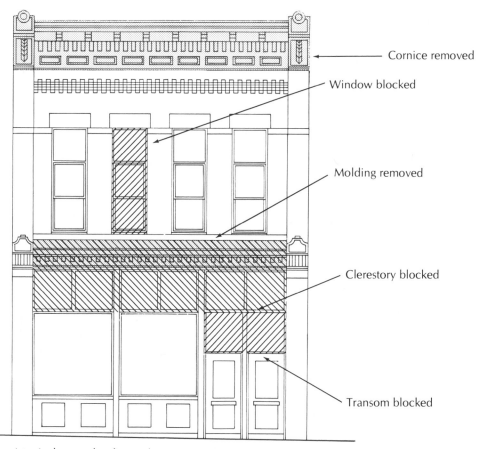

Cornice removed

Window blocked

Molding removed

Clerestory blocked

Transom blocked

A typical example of a patch-up approach

crucial element in a general effort to improve store business or business in a whole downtown district. Facade design can boost the image of a store, but the goal of improving sales requires a combination of efforts such as facade design, interior design, merchandise selection, display advertising, and management. Facade improvement should not be seen as a panacea to retail problems, but rather as an important factor, taken in conjunction with these other factors in improving business on Main Street. The success stories in this chapter attest to the validity of this approach.

Five factors are significant in evaluating a facade renovation project: 1) the sensibilities of the owner and his commitment to the renovation project, 2) the construction and design quality of the original facade, 3) the size of the budget, 4) the resources available in terms of design advice, materials, and skilled workmen, and 5) the relationship between owner and tenant, if these are not the same, concerning who is reponsibile for the building's appearance and upkeep.

The combination of reasons for renovation and these five factors determines the scope and design of the work undertaken. Most reservations fall into one of three categories as outlined below.

The Patch-Up Approach

This method of renovation is not a comprehensive or planned approach. Over a period of years, the building owner commissions unrelated repairs or modifications as needed, which are carried out by a variety of workmen. Although this approach is not inherently bad, it usually fails to consider the overall design of the building and the effect of the accumulated alterations. In the course of successive renovations, signs are tacked onto the facade with little regard for placement or size, and portions of the building's details are covered. Deteriorating ornaments are simply removed. The ground floor is painted or otherwise refinished without regard for the upper portion of the facade, and usually with no eye toward neighboring buildings on the street.

One of the most common—and unfortunate—patch-up alterations is the blocking of a part of the display windows, usually the upper clerestory. In many late nineteenth-century build-

ings the ceilings were originally fourteen or more feet higher, and these upper portions of glass helped introduce light into the sizeable space. The modernization of many buildings, though, has included the installation of air conditioning and recessed lighting, and secondary ceilings have been installed to hide the necessary mechanical equipment. In order to hide the alterations from the street the clerestory is closed in with plywood or stucco. Such alterations disturb the original character of the building by changing the proportions and facade elements and thus disrupt the visual continuity of the street.

If a new tenant moves into the building and modifies the space to suit a different sort of business, the alterations are even more dramatic. A typical problem occurs when a first-floor shop space is converted into a bar or cinema. Both uses require lower light levels, and so the large display windows are entirely blocked. These photographs of Buena Vista, Colorado, illustrate several victims of the patch-up approach.

The New Image Approach

Unlike the patch-up approach, which is not comprehensive enough, the new image approach is *too* comprehensive. In accordance with one of several

When storefronts are adapted to new uses, an often erroneous decision is made to make drastic changes to the building, such as the way the shop windows were removed and new doors installed for this movie house.

themes, the building is suddenly and completely altered, often by an overlay that entirely obscures the original facade.

Overscaled colonial details create a new—and unbecoming—image for this Victorian store.

Exotic themes are often tried in an attempt to dress up an old building. Ironically, the original details of the second story are much more interesting and could have contributed to the marketing image of the restaurant below.

Perhaps the most common is the historic theme. The facade is pseudo-antiqued by the use of materials and stylistic elements that connote an earlier period: the "Colonial" and "Wild West" styles are popular choices. Another theme is the Exotic, in which the intent is to establish a foreign setting. Restaurants that want a building exterior that reflects their menu frequently choose this approach, and an ordinary brick facade may suddenly become Polynesian. The themes vary from town to town, but the results are similar. Authenticity and historic accuracy are hardly concerns of this approach, in which thematic elements are caricatured beyond their original proportions in order to fit the facade. The results are often bewildering as well as less than becoming.

Another new image approach strives to make the building appear more contemporary. Metal or other slick cladding covers the facade in order to create a streamlined effect, as was done to the firehouse in Fort Collins, Colorado. In an expensive bit of corrective surgery, the windows were realigned at

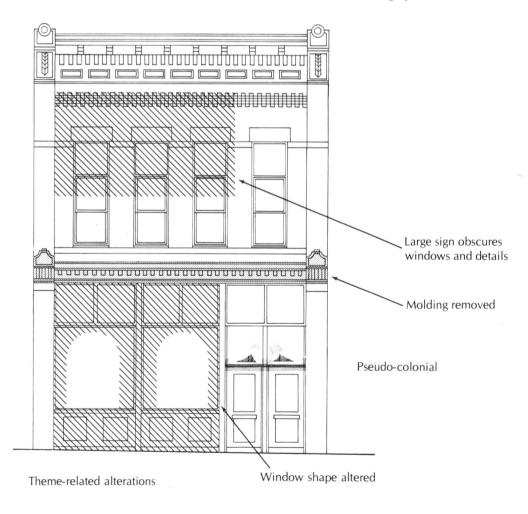

Large sign obscures windows and details

Molding removed

Pseudo-colonial

Theme-related alterations

Window shape altered

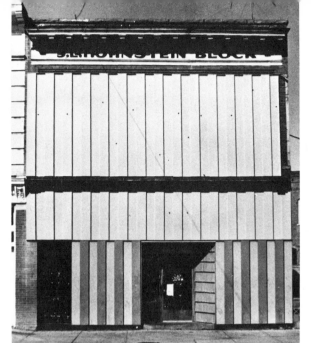

The firehouse in Fort Collins, Colorado, enclosed in a corrugated metal straitjacket.

The tin-canning of Main Street is dramatically demonstrated here in Fort Collins, Colorado, where the Hohnstein Block was held captive for many years.

that time in order to make the facade appear more uniform. This tin-canning of Main Street buildings swept the country in the 1950's and 1960's and is still, unfortunately, a popular option.

The new image approach often involves substantial alterations to the underlying original facade. Cornices, brackets, and other details that project too much to be covered are stripped away, while details such as brick arches are elminated and replaced by the cleaner look of steel beams. Since the assumption is that the new image is there to stay, there is little concern for the original facade. In fact, the old face

is sometimes damaged so extensively by the renovation that it is beyond the point of return.

Merchants choose the new image approach thinking that it will be an inexpensive solution to cracked masonry or decaying ornamentation. The applied veneer does not, however, solve these problems; it merely conceals them. As mentioned above, the installation of the weighty cover-up layer can actually accelerate the facade deterioration, although such new problems are similarly concealed. Finally, the new image is in reality more expensive than other options. Merchants are willing to

pay the high cost of materials and installation because they expect the new facade will endure, but actually it often requires a substantial maintanance and repair budget in addition to increasing the repair costs of the hidden facade.

In all of the new look approaches, whether historic, exotic, or contemporary, the underlying assumption is that the original facade is not worth preserving. Coupled with this notion is a failure to see a distinction between a Main Street shop and a new, highwayside franchise. Merchants feel that in order to compete with these more recent stores the Main Street shops must

After metal cladding is removed, damage to cornice, lintels, and other decorative features is evident.

With the cladding gone, original features of the Hohnstein Bloc are once more visible. Renovation is under way on the storefront.

evaluate their appearance, and owners turn to the same plastic signs, industrialized building materials and slick finishes. But Main Street was built to appeal to the pedestrian, while the strip was built to grab the attention of the highway driver at forty-five miles per hour. What works for one does not necessarily work for the other. Most Main Streets already have some underlying architectural distinction, and a richness of detail that is meant for pedestrian viewing; it is easier and far more successful to achieve a cohesive image by sympathetic rehabilitation than by attempting to smother it with a new image. The enhancement approach is a good method for these Main Street facades.

The Enhancement Approach

The approach that most preservationists favor is one that retains as much as possible of the original facade. Architectural details are accentuated, while complimentary new details are added. In this manner changes are incorporated but, unlike the patch-up approach, each detail is carefully designed to contribute to a unified whole.

Preserving the building as it originally appeared is one option within this approach, and certainly an acceptable one, but often this is not possible. Typically, over the years some elements have been lost or damaged or the building has been altered structurally. It may not be feasible or even desirable, given costs and new uses, to strive for historic authenticity. The task instead is to rehabilitate in keeping with the building's character while accommodating current use.

The enhancement approach often involves removing years of additions, although some caution should be exercised here. In some instances much of a building's character is derived from these additions which, although not original to the building, may have come to characterize the facade or the business located there. A particular sign, door or ornament may have a certain quality worth preserving, and its removal would result in a loss of identity. The Art Deco sign on the Federal style Fowle's Drugs is one such later addition that was considered integral to the building today and was accordingly retained as was the wooden Indian or the Leavitt and Peirce facade.

Enhancement is usually less expen-

The typical storefront of the turn of the century contained large expanses of glass, usually divided into two sections. Columns and pilasters established the vertical limits of the facade, and the whole storefront was capped with ornamental molding. At the base of the storefront, panels covered the area below the display platforms. The entry was easily identified because of its recessed position.

sive than a new image, since the existing facade serves as the basis for the design and the stripping off and adding on are thus minimized. The enhancement approach does, however, require an analysis of the building's architectural components, the restoration or recreation of some elements and a conscientious maintenance of the facade. A typical building and its component parts, as well as some of the techniques frequently required by this type of renovation, are described below.

The Typical Commercial Facade

No two facades are precisely alike, and a number of influences—geography, climate, building traditions, available materials, architects and workers—account for the variety across the country. Nevertheless, there are certain characteristics that the surviving Main Street buildings have in common. A typical commercial building may date from the 1880's or 1890's, when a thriving economy produced a coast-to-coast building boom and durable materials were used. This prototype is of brick, stone, or cast iron and stands two or three stories high. On the ground floor is a retail business. As

originally constructed, the second floor sometimes served as the shop keeper's apartment or it was leased as office space; today it is often vacant. There is a distinct visual difference between the two stories. While the first floor is almost transparent, the second floor is contained and solid. The difference in how the floors were used accounts for their respective appearances. Large panes of glass, separated by thin structural members, allowed for shop displays on the ground floor level. Above, the owner's quarters or office space instead had a number of smaller windows, regularly spaced in a well-defined wall.

The storefront has similarly standardized components. At the bottom is a base panel, frequently of wood, that serves as a kickplate. Above the kickplate is the glass of the main display window. Often this large expanse of glass is subdivided by a horizontal framing member, creating a transom of clerestory glass in the upper portion. The clerestory is capped with a horizontal, usually projecting, molding, and above this molding the store sign is frequently mounted, although the sign is sometimes integrated into the horizontal band itself.

These two storefronts in Durango, Colorado exhibit the traditional components of commercial facades, although they have experienced minor changes. The lower level is distinctly different from the upper story, in that it is quite transparent and light, whereas the second floor appears more solid. An ornamental cornice caps the building.

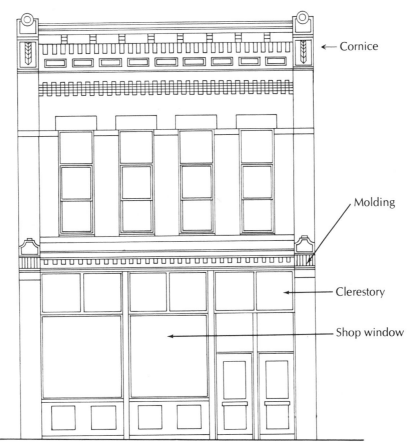

← Cornice

Molding

Clerestory

Shop window

Typical commercial facade in original condition

Brown's Cigar Store in Corning, New York: a good example of a late 19th-century storefront.

Standard additions to the typical storefront are signs and awnings. Notice how the awnings on the upper story windows accentuate the pattern of the spaced windows. Ornamental details, especially along the edges of the facade, are also common.

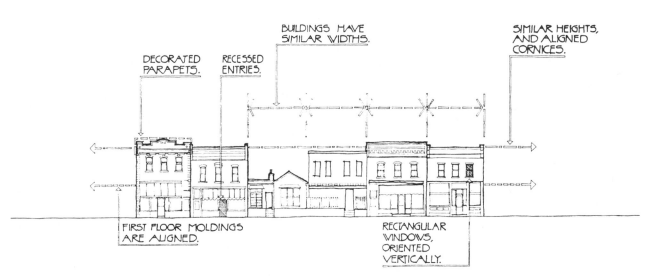

Durango Block, Colorado, showing unity of street.

The shop entrance is recessed from the storefront plane, and the sides of the display windows lead to the entrance. In older buildings these windows are set at an obtuse angle, creating a funnel toward the entrance, while in storefronts erected or modernized since the 1950's the side windows are more commonly perpendicular to the facade. The recessed area provides shelter to patrons in bad weather and allows space for the door to swing outward without disrupting sidewalk traffic, a convention that is now required by most building codes. The darkness of this recess visually signifies "entry" even without the often obvious signs that point to it.

Additions to the basic facade are typically awnings, canopies, window boxes, architectural ornaments and shutters. Each of these elements can serve to emphasize the lines and shapes of the facade itself. Awnings, for example, reinforce the visual separation of the ground-floor display windows

from the second story, while window boxes and shutters emphasize the spacing pattern of the windows. Ornamental cornices and capitals accentuate framing pieces or define the outline of the building.

Although somewhat simplified, these basic facade characteristics still apply to most modern storefronts. When the majority of the buildings on a Main Street have these similar components, the street scene has a visual continuity and strong quality of cohesion. If one or more buildings disturb these characteristics, the entire street may suffer.

The enhancement approach takes into consideration the overall character of the street and seeks to enhance its continuity. Just as buildings have common components, so do most Main Streets. One of the strongest features is the alignment of cornices, window sills, and other elements, creating strong horizontal lines that lead the eye from building to building. Long rectangular signs, mounted along the tops of

the ground-level storefronts, also contribute to this horizontal continuity. Other unifying patterns are created by the recesses of regularly-spaced windows and less-frequent doorways, ornaments such as brackets and dentils, and building materials such as clapboards, bricks, and cast iron columns.

Not all Main Streets have buildings of a single style, and even those that do were probably not designed with visual continuity in mind—buildings on streets built up in boom periods simply share the style that was vogue. Nevertheless, nineteenth-century limitations of building materials and methods created a fairly restricted vocabulary of facade designs, and the resulting visual coherence, an arrangement of spaces, shapes, and textures, created a unified cityscape.

Today, the available range of styles, materials and technology is much broader, and rehabilitations and new designs must be more carefully considered if they are to be compatible on

Though styles are not identical, similarities of height, cornice line, and facade rhythms create a unified streetscape.

An oversized and misplaced sign.

Main Street. The continuity of the street can be reinforced by working within a vocabulary developed from existing characteristics. The guidelines that follow are not a formula for commercial rehabilitation, but they do address the issue of visual coherence and present some solutions to problems commonly encountered when renovating facades.

SIGNS

A sign is often the primary identifying feature of a business, the link between a building's exterior and the business inside. A good sign can help a business by making it distinctive. It pinpoints a store's location on the street and makes the business easy to find, creates an attractive image for the store, and encourages passers-by to venture inside.

Many merchants, however, do not know what criteria to apply when selecting a sign. Some believe that bigger is better and choose the largest which the traveling sign salesman can foist upon them; others believe that one type is as good as another and seek out the

A sign properly scaled to the storefront.

least expensive example. The result is a clutter of poorly-designed signs that not only disfigure the street but also fail to convey the desired information. Typical is the mass-produced white plastic panel, illuminated from fluorescent tubes inside, with the store's name and often that of a corporate sponsor painted or formed on the front. The price of these signs makes them popular, but they have several disadvantages. These failings are apparent when one considers three important aspects of signs: the size and position of the sign, its design and materials, and its illumination.

Size and Position—Since it is mass-produced, the common white plastic sign comes in a limited number of shapes and sizes. The sign dimensions do not relate to the facade and, when mounted, the sign is obviously an afterthought rather than an integrated part of the storefront. A sign that is individually designed for a specific storefront creates a more cohesive facade.

Merchants should analyze their storefronts and ascertain where a sign would best fit, and the location will determine the range of acceptable shapes and sizes for the sign. Typical locations are flat, unornamented surfaces often found directly above the display windows, door, or second-story windows, or in a pediment at the top of the building. Some facades have several such acceptable locations which are intended for signs. The key to selecting a size and proportion compatible with the facade is to confine the sign to one of those areas and remember that bigger is *not* always better, especially when an oversize sign obscures architectural details.

Another type of sign is one that projects from the facade. Large projecting signs only create an additional clutter, and some towns have banned this type of sign entirely. Where allowed, though, small projecting signs can be effective and can actually enhance the image of the street. The nature of the sign may eliminate the need for excessive lettering, and many merchants have found that traditional trade symbol signs, such as those in the shape of clocks, shoes, or books, are sufficient. Research psychologists even report that symbols are recognized and transferred to long-term memory faster than written ones, so symbols make good advertising sense.

A carved projecting sign and awnings add character to this Main Street store.

Projecting signs can convey information by their shape alone.

107

Materials and Design—A custom made sign, rather than a mass-produced one, can take advantage of a wide range of materials and flexibility of styles. The entire sign can be formed into a shape, or, in the case of a wooden sign, symbols as well as letters can be carved into the surface. Individual letters can be applied directly to the facade or can be painted, stencilled or engraved on windows. The variety of colors, typefaces and designs is unlimited, but too much information and variety detracts from the sign's message. Simplicity should be the goal.

Many materials are suitable for signs, including wood, metal, plexiglass, plastic, and fabric. Plastic is popular because of its low cost, but problems of maintenance and inflexibility more than outweigh this initial advantage. Any repairs or addition of information—such as a name change—necessitate the replacement of a plastic sign, as paint will peel off. Often the light boxes inside the plastic form break down. Flush plastic letters in a wooden panel with external spot lights are probably the best solution if plastic is desired. Other materials which are more adaptable, such as wood, may therefore be less expensive over the long run, as well as more in keeping with the character of an older building.

A merchant can design his own sign but it is often more successful to employ an experienced designer or craftsman. If the materials are carefully chosen and the design shows a bit of ingenuity, the resulting sign will be a considerable improvement over the plastic box. A good example discussed in this chapter's case studies is Hattie's Dress Shop sign. This creative, carved wooden sign replaced a nondescript plastic panel, and it cost six hundred dollars in 1977.

Illumination—Illumination can come from either inside or outside the sign. Both types of lighting are acceptable, depending upon the size of the sign and the other light available. Neon, for example, is an internally-lit type of sign that can be very effective if used in small quantities. The white plastic panel sign is also illuminated from the inside, but these signs are often quite large and have the disadvantage of overwhelming the facade or the lighting of the shop windows. Internally-lit plastic signs also present such difficulties in replacing fluorescent tubes that

This new stained glass, in the clerestory, illustrates how the work of local craftsmen can be integrated into facade renovation. The windows show the food served inside. Here in Staunton, Virginia, a local preservation organization, Historic Staunton Inc., has provided design service to merchants. Their work is supported by community development block grants and includes the acquisition of facade easement.

merchants have burned-out tubes in far too long, creating a bad image for the store. Often, then, it is more effective if the sign is illuminated by an external source. Spot lights directed toward the sign illuminate portions of the building as well as the sign, and it is possible to balance the color and intensity of the light with that in the display windows. When no other light is available, the internally-lit sign tends to dominate the facade—sometimes cutting it in two.

PAINT

A fresh coat of paint on doors and trim, and sometimes on an entire facade, is good for a building's appearance and essential for its upkeep. Surfaces must be prepared by removing old paint, and color schemes should be carefully considered. While a single color does provide a unified appearance

it can also obscure the modlings, brackets and cornices that make a facade distinctive. A better solution is to paint these details in a contrasting, complementary color. The balance of background and highlighted detail depends upon the individual facade; too little detail can be bland, while too much can be overwhelming. As a rule, surfaces such as brick that are still unpainted should remain so.

Color choice is largely a matter of personal taste, but the colors should be appropriate to the building materials and style and to other buildings on the block. Usually, very bright colors and garish combinations should be avoided where they will contrast too strongly with adjacent buildings and no more than two or three colors should be used, to keep the scheme simple. Local preservation groups can sometimes provide specific suggestions of colors appro-

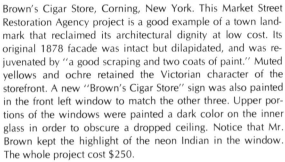

Brown's Cigar Store, Corning, New York. This Market Street Restoration Agency project is a good example of a town landmark that reclaimed its architectural dignity at low cost. Its original 1878 facade was intact but dilapidated, and was rejuvenated by "a good scraping and two coats of paint." Muted yellows and ochre retained the Victorian character of the storefront. A new "Brown's Cigar Store" sign was also painted in the front left window to match the other three. Upper portions of the windows were painted a dark color on the inner glass in order to obscure a dropped ceiling. Notice that Mr. Brown kept the highlight of the neon Indian in the window. The whole project cost $250.

priate to the region and building style. If authenticity is desired, the original color scheme of a facade can be determined by scraping off layers of paint in a test patch, allowing for discoloration.

Ornaments and Details—Decorative wooden moldings and brackets are usually the first casualties of facade deterioration. Their elaborate surfaces expose more of the material to weathering processes, and further decay occurs if moisture seeps in at the wall joints. It is better to correct the conditions that allow decay and to repair these features than cover them over, as the deterioration otherwise simply continues beneath the sheet metal or other siding.

Some ornaments may already be missing, and replicas can be fabricated from the original material, such as wood or metal, or modern materials can be substituted. Simple details can be fabricated from vacuum-formed plastic and painted to match the original. More elaborate ornaments can be made from fiberglass. Iron and steel ornaments, such as railings, may be replaced with aluminum if rust is a problem. If the cost of replicating a detail is too high

for the renovation budget, a simplified design based on the original forms can be devised. (Sometimes detailing can even be simulated by a clever paint job; see the story of Mr. Pawn Shop for such an example.)

Cleaning—Facades constructed of brick, stone, or masonry may warrant the removal of dirt or paint for cosmetic reasons. Cleaning a facade can visually bring it back to life but, if done improperly, it can also damage the material and cause structural problems. The best plan is to seek out a competent cleaning contractor who can evaluate the particular building and suggest a cleaning method. Whichever method he recommends should first be tried on a four-to-six-square-foot test patch, and this exposed surface should be allowed to weather for a period of one week to several months. This test is the best way to ascertain if the cleaning will cause any long-term problems.

If a cleaning method is too severe, it will remove not only the dirt and paint but also the outer surface of the construction material, especially of brick. Sandblasting should never be used, for this reason. The abrasive action of

sandblasting causes the brick to lose its glaze and become porous, allowing dirt and water to seep in. Alternative methods of cleaning involve water, sometimes in conjunction with detergent and scrubbing, and chemical solutions. These are usually safer methods but they, too, can be harsh at times.

Maintenance—Wooden surfaces, such as doors and cornices, should be painted as often as necessary to keep the surface sealed. Brick and stone facades also require periodic maintenance, primarily mortar repair. The mortar used in older buildings is commonly a composition of sand and lime, a mixture that gradually erodes as drainage water from the roof and projections runs over the wall. Water and dirt can work their way in through eroded mortar just as they can through porous brick, and periodically the mortar should be patched by a process known as repointing or tuckpointing. Repointing is not a frequent need; once every fifty to seventy-five years is usually sufficient, and it is a small price for the continued life of an older building.

Whittemore Block, Arlington, Massachusetts. In an effort to improve the commercial image of this Boston suburb, the town offered free design assistance to owners interested in facade improvements. The Whittemore Block across from the town library was a typically cluttered series of storefronts, and the first to undergo renovation. Although the facade itself has few distinguishing characteristics, removal of the clumsy signs and accretions under the direction of townscape planner Ronald Lee Fleming, created a more unified, inviting perspective. Painted wooden signs fit into the proper scale, while awnings and bronzed glass help reduce the intensity of a southern exposure.

Teddy's Lunch, Portsmouth, New Hampshire. When new owners Paul and Christine Rampon bought Teddy's Lunch in 1978, they thought the front "lacked vitality." Using their own designs and labor, they painted the facade Newport Blue and white and installed a matching awning. They contributed some landscaping while the city, in a general renewal of the adjacent market square, added brick sidewalks and benches. Impressed, the owner of the entire building sandblasted the structure (not usually a recommended technique; see p. 109), revealing its original brick and creating a pleasant contrast with the neighboring building. Total cost was $470: $390 for the awning, $30 in paint, $50 in landscaping, and the Rampons' labor.

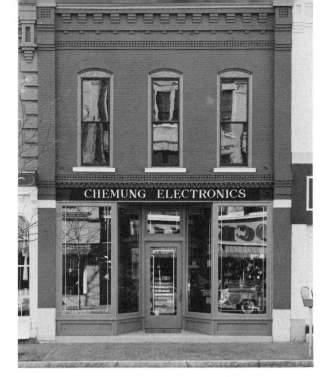

Chemung Electronics, Corning, New York. Owner Mike Semel joined many other Market Street merchants in deciding to renovate his facade in 1975. The 1880 facade on his store was intact except for the cutting down of windows for increased sign area in the 1960's. New plate glass windows of the original size were installed and a smaller, handcrafted sign in gold leaf replaced the plastic lettering. As a result, Chemung Electronics' storefront is lighter and more inviting, with increased window space and a less cluttered look. Painting of the brick in deep red gives the facade a more dignified look; lighter shades emphasize window ornament, sills, and kickplates. Total cost was $3,200 in 1977: $400 for the sign, $500 for paint, and $2,300 for windows and frames.

It is important to repoint with a mortar that approximates the original color and hardness. Portland cement, known for its durability and strength, is often used as a mortar, but it can do more harm than good. Since the cement is harder than the bricks, the two do not expand and contract at the same rate during cycles of freezing and thawing or daytime heating and nighttime cooling. The bricks must give instead of the mortar, and they crack and spall, or scale, as a result. A consultant or contractor can recommend a mortar that better adjusts to the wall's dynamics. When replacing damaged brick the new should similarly match the old in hardness and, if unpainted, in color.

The best way to minimize maintenance of masonry walls is to make sure that gutters and downspouts are doing their job. A good roof, sound eaves, and proper sealing at the joints are the best protection.

Harold's Army and Navy Store, Corning, New York. This 1930 Art Deco storefront, built for Corning's first supermarket, presented an attractive contrast to the Victorian streetscape of Market Street, but by 1974 it had decayed severely. Many of the light green carrara glass panels were cracked, and an out-of-scale sign contributed to a general look of shabbiness. Under the guidance of Market Street Restoration Agency Director Norman Mintz, a restoration project was begun, aimed at renewing the Art Deco appeal at low cost. Since carrara glass was too expensive, Mintz substituted wood panels painted shiny black underneath the windows. A Deco-lettered sign replaced the block-lettered one, and valances were added to the inner windows for an attractive lighting effect. Black awnings help to unify the facade. Total cost was $1,800.

Hattie's Dress Store, Chelsea, Massachusetts. The old Hattie's before downtown revitalization incentive encouraged the owner to strip off the yellow shingles and oversized corrugated plastic sign.

The new Hattie's. A handcrafted wooden sign—the first on the block—ceramic titles below the windows, and subdued coloring give Hattie's an inviting look, more akin to a women's dress store than its earlier likeness. The sign carved by Ken Amidon reflects the fabric of a woman's dress and cost $600, with $300 paid by the city using community development funds. The facade cost $1400. The city contributed $350; total cost to the owner was $1350 in 1978.

Mister Pawn Shop, Fort Collins, Colorado. This new business has made the best of a modest shopfront by recalling the structure's original details, yet without actually reconstructing them. When Mr. Ted Will purchased the premises in 1978, the building had been stripped of all its original detail, the brick facade had been covered with stucco, and a metal canopy cut off the store front from the upper half of the building. Historic research revealed that the original building, built in the 1890's, had cast iron pilasters flanking the facade. The architect Nore Winter proposed a paint scheme that simulated the original vertical and horizontal bands, but in an abstraction of the original. Other changes were also implemented: a new awning was installed where an earlier one was known to have existed, and a new wooden sign incorporated the established logo for Mister Pawn Shop. The facade measures twenty feet across and eighteen feet high. Acting as his own project administrator, and providing much of the labor, Ted Will completed the project in 1978 for less than $1,000. This renovation has encouraged other merchants to undertake similar projects in the historic district of Fort Collins.

Downtown Montpelier, Vermont. This business block in downtown Montpelier illustrates several different approaches toward facade improvement. The hardware store, supported by city funds, did the mock restoration on the left. Although based on a townscape design plan prepared by a local architect, the machine-made look is precisely that—aluminum instead of wooden clapboards, and brackets on the cornice which look too thin. The old Brown Brothers Insurance Company in the middle, by contrast shows how a new material, annodized aluminum with a bronze finish now cladding the clerestory windows can complement the original cast iron columns. By setting the newer, broader windows back behind the columns, the rhythm of the facade apertures is maintained more successfully than in the hardware store on the left. The radiator grille on the right was part of the 60's corporate cover up, and, true to form, it is a bank.

FINANCING

Financing facade renovations is often the most difficult element in Main Street projects. Absentee landlords, marginal businesses, and conservative shopkeepers all contribute to a reluctance to change the status quo, no matter how tawdry it may be. Financial incentives combined with on-the-street design guidance can accelerate successful results within a short period of time. In the last ten years, a number of creative approaches to this problem have been devised in various parts of the country. The proper package of financing will depend on the scale and specific situation of the building, as well as an overall analysis of the condition of the street.

Many cities and towns have set up facade renovation programs providing loans well below the prime lending rate; this usually involves local banks and sometimes a non-profit economic development corporation that initiates the program with federal money. For example, the Lowell Development Corporation has loaned over one million dollars since 1976 on thirty-six facade projects in this Massachusetts mill city. Such loans can vary from as little as 6% interest to as much as two points below the prime rate.

Often these programs were established using federal funds such as Community Development Block Grants (CDBG) or Urban Development Action Grants (UDAG). With the future availability of such funds in doubt, alternative means will have to be devised.

Some Things Not To Do With Your Main Street Facade

These selections represent a cross-section of Main Street coverups, from mansard shingle to Colonial clapboard. In each case, the store owners would have been much better off spending their money on a renovation that respected the character of the original building design.

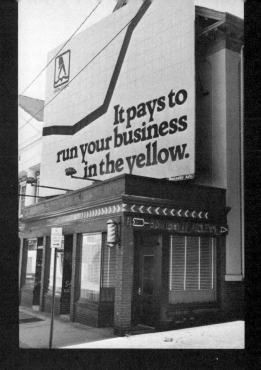

Massachusetts is one state that has enacted a program similar to the UDAG program to offset the loss of federal funds. Increasingly, though, private sector dollars will have to be used to finance low interest loan pools for storefront renovations. Williamsport, Pennsylvania created a $500,000 pool with half of the funds coming from the Williamsport Foundation, a large private philanthropic organization, and the other half from three local banks. The average interest rate on loans from this fund was 6% in 1981, combining 12% and interest-free loans.

The 1981 Economic Recovery Tax Act includes several provisions which will assist private financing of facade renovations. Owners may take tax credits of up to 25% or 5-year amortization on the cost of a significant rehabilitation of a historic structure. To qualify as "significant," the cost of the rehabilitation must be more than the adjusted basis of the property or $5,000, whichever is greater. Clearly, these incentives will be must useful to proprietors carrying out major interior renovations as well as facade renovations.

Another method of financing involved facade easements. Easements are legal restrictions placed on the exterior (or interior) of a building for a specified period of time, usually for perpetuity. Historic Annapolis, Inc., a private, non-profit organization in Maryland, was one of the first to initiate such a program to enhance the handsome early structures of their capital. Using a revolving fund, the corporation buys an easement for perpetuity on a property; the property owner uses this money toward facade restoration. Historic Annapolis supplies architectural research and preliminary restoration advice. Most of these easements cost less than $5,000. Under the terms of the easement, no changes can be made to the property and no resale can be made without the permission of Historic Annapolis. Their program has been so successful—nearly 40 facade improvements since 1969—that the state of Maryland has instituted a similar program, offering to buy easements up to $20,000 in other Maryland towns. Another method to make facade easements attractive to property owners has been applied in Philadelphia. The owners can donate the right to control the

appearance of their facades to the Philadelphia Historic Preservation Corporation, a non-profit organization. The appraised value of the easement can then be claimed as a charitable deduction for federal tax purposes.

In Annapolis, the easement program is not limited to historic buildings, though most of the facade renovations are within the historic district. It extends to vacant land and to buildings of no architectural significance in order to protect the character of adjacent historic areas.

The major benefit of buying easements as a policy tool is the ability to use public funds to improve the appearance of private property. If the ownership of the easement did not rest in public hands this benefit could not be achieved. However, the administration of these programs is often better accomplished by private preservation groups, who initally applied the pressure to secure such programs and who find staff dedicated to the conscientious implementation of the facade renovations.

Often, easements will be given to a municipal body in exchange for financial assistance on facade renovation. If a city or state is interested in preserving the character of a district that does not have historic district status, easements are a good way to insure that facades will not be changed. Portland, Maine set aside $77,000 of a major UDAG grant for this purpose. The city offers merchants in the downtown either 25% of total renovation costs or $10,000, whichever is less, in exchange for a seven-year easement on the building. Greater Portland Landmarks, Inc., a private, non-profit preservation organization, has coordinated a design review committee for the city. By 1982, twelve projects have been completed under the program.

However, the donation of easements requires an assessment of the difference in value between the property with the facade preserved (usually preserving the property as it is) and the highest and best use for the land. In older downtowns such as Staunton, Virginia, where a private preservation organization, Historic Staunton, Inc., has assisted property owners on forty one of approximately one hundred twenty five facades on Beverly Street, director Kathleen Frazier, thinks that the do-

nation requirements are a burden. It is difficult to prove under the existing rules that there is a higher value which could be realized on downtown property without restriction as compared to well located shopping centers on the outskirts.

Now easements are even more attractive financially to owners as a result of changes in the 1980 tax act. Tax deductions are available to those property owners who donate easements in perpetuity to qualified charitable organizations "exclusively for conservation purposes." Such organizations usually charge a fee to cover the administrative costs of the process; this ranges from the $50 charged by the Foundation for San Francisco's Architectural Heritage to the 10% of easement value charged by the L'Enfant Trust of Washington, D.C. Often, such programs are not well advertised. Call a local or state preservation office to see whether such opportunities exist in a particular community.

Communites can use the governmental tool of a taking by eminent domain as a basis for facade renovation programs where absentee landlords and the need to generate local merchant leadership make the voluntary purchase or donation less feasible but in Buffalo, New York, the city's community development agency insured a very comprehensive treatment of storefronts in a three block area of the Grant-Ferry business district by first sending in a building inspector to list violations. Then the city offered to acquire the easements which released the property owner from liability for the facade repairs. The agency achieved a hundred percent compliance with seven year restricted covenant to insure merchants' maintenance of the facade. The work was funded with community development block grant and executed by private architects (see photo in the Introduction).

One deterrent to facade improvement is the owner's fear of higher property tax assessments afterward. Oregon has instituted a highly successful program whereby tax assessments are frozen for 15 years on buildings that have been historically rehabilitated. Chelsea, Massachusetts, when it embarked on an important downtown revitalization program, enacted a similar 5-year freeze. Financial incentives for facade renovations appear to be gathering momentum as more cities and states see the benefits of such a program.

Chelsea devised some other features that, collectively, served as important incentives to merchants thinking about renovations:

— subsidizing 25% of facade improvements up to $2,000, and 50% of new sign costs; (for more quality control)
— free sign design by the consultant team, as well as free sign take-down and temporary sign installation;
— two local banks offering loans on facade improvements at 8% interest;
— improvements in sidewalks, lighting, landscaping, and street furniture.

Usually it is a combination of elements such as these that makes facade improvements feasible. The right mix of elements depends on the needs and resources of the community. In the last ten years, so many innovative ways of financing facade renovations have been devised that there is likely to be an appropriate solution for any individual project.

Glossary of
Facade Terms

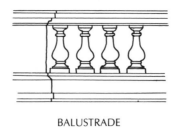

BALUSTRADE

BRACKET

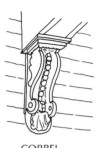

CORBEL

Architrave — A plain horizontal band in the entablature, situated above the capital and below the frieze.

Art Deco — A term originating about 1960 that refers to the style of art and architecture popular between WWI and WWII, characterized by streamlined forms, geometric patterns, boldness, and simplicity. A good example is the Chrysler Building in New York.

Art Moderne — A style popular from 1930–1945, emphasizing curved, streamlined forms. Ornamentation relies heavily on mirrors, metal elements, and low relief around doorways. Art Moderne was widely used in bus stations of the time.

Art Nouveau — A term referring to the style of art and architecture popular during the period 1880–1910, characterized by curved, slender, elegant line, the most frequent motif of which was the lily; the style was especially popular in France.

Balustrade — A series of balusters, upright or often vase-shaped, supports for a rail.

Beltcourse — A narrow horizontal band projecting from the exterior walls of a building, usually defining the interior floor levels.

Bracket — A support element under eaves, shelves or other overhangs; often more decorative than functional.

Buttress — A vertical structure, attached to a wall for supporting or giving stability to a wall or building.

Cantilever — A projecting beam or part of a structure supported only at one end.

Capital — The top decorated member of a column or pilaster crowning the shaft and supporting the entablature.

Cast Iron — Iron, shaped in a mold, that is brittle, hard, and cannot be welded; often used in late 19th-century commercial facades.

Clerestory — In a church, the upper part of the nave walls, usually pierced by windows; in a commercial building, the upper part of the main floor shopwindows.

Colonial — A term referring to the style of many 18th-century buildings, characterized by plain brick or shingle facades, narrow sash windows, large chimneys, gable roofs, and an ornamented doorway often with pilasters and a triangular pediment; frequently and popularly revived.

Corbel — A masonry bracket projecting from the face of a wall that generally supports a cornice, beam or arch.

Corinthian — The most ornate of the classical Greek orders of architecture, characterized by a slender fluted column with a bell-shaped capital decorated with stylized acanthus leaves; used extensively by the Romans.

Cornice — The projecting horizontal ornamental unit along the top of a building, wall, or entablature.

Doric — The simplest of the classical Greek orders, characterized by heavy fluted columns with no base, plain saucer-shaped capitals and a bold simple cornice. Roman Doric columns have bases but no fluting.

Entablature — The horizontal ensemble resting on top of columns or pilasters, consisting of the architrave, frieze, and cornice.

Fascia — A plain horizontal face board or panel beneath the eaves.

Federal — A style popular in the late 18th and early 19th centuries, characterized by a low pitched roof, smooth facade, and often an elliptical fan light over doorways with slender flanking side lights; more advanced than Colonial yet more restrained than Georgian.

Frieze — A horizontal band of sculpture in bas-relief used as ornament between the architrave and the cornice.

Gable — The triangular wall segments at the end of a double-pitch, or gable roof.

Gothic Revival — A style popular in the early and mid-19th century which covered a broad range of attempts to recall medieval styles in architecture; often used elements of English Gothic with pointed arches, gabled windows, tall spires, and elaborate, heavy decoration.

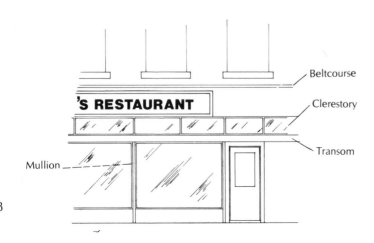

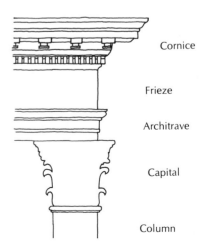

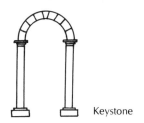

Keystone

MANSARD ROOF

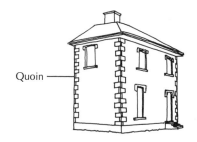

Quoin

Hip Roof — A roof which has slopes of the same pitch rising from all four sides of a building.

Ionic — One of the classical orders of architecture, characterized by scroll capitals.

Italianate — A style popular during the mid and late 19th century which revived elements from Italian architecture ranging from medieval to Baroque; often characterized by overhanging eaves with elaborate brackets, low roofs, corner quoins, and a cupola or tower. It was widely used in cast iron commercial facades.

Keystone — The central stone of an arch or vault; often accentuated or carved.

Lintel — A horizontal beam bridging an opening. Post and lintel construction refers to the use of posts and beams for support.

Mansard Roof — A roof with a steep lower pitch and a flatter pitch above; popular in French Second Empire style.

Modern Movement — A style of architecture popular from the 1930's to the present, exemplifying the philosophy "form follows function," characterized by such building technologies as highrise, reinforced concrete, extreme cantilevers, reflective glass facades, curtain walls and the lack of decoration. Often referred to as "International Style" after a 1932 exhibition in New York.

Mullion — A vertical post dividing a window into two or more parts.

Neoclassical — Pertaining to the revival of the styles of ancient Greek and Roman architecture, a movement especially popular in the United States from 1810–1850 and 1890–1930, and often used for public buildings.

Pediment — A wide, low-pitched gable surmounting a facade, doorway, or window, often employed in Neoclassical or Neocolonial facades.

Pilaster — A shallow pier attached to a wall, decorated to resemble a classical column.

Polychromy — The use of many colors in decoration.

Quoin — Blocks of stone or brick used to accentuate the corners of a building.

Romanesque Revival — A style popular in the mid to late 19th century, employing semicircular arches over windows and doorways, decorated corbels, and often square towers. Richardsonian Romanesque derived from the work of H.H. Richardson (1838–1886), emphasizing massivity, heavy entryway arches, and horizontal profile.

Rustication — Masonry cut in massive blocks separated from each other by deep joints.

Sash Window — A window with the panes of glass set into a frame which can be moved up and down; most commonly associated with Colonial or Federal styles.

Second Empire — An elaborate style, popular in the late 19th century, notable for mansard roofs, blocklike shape emphasized by quoins, and central towers.

Soffit — The underside of an architectural element.

Stringcourse — A narrow, continuous ornamental band set into a building.

Terra Cotta — A fine-grained, brownred, fired clay used extensively for decoration in the 19th century.

Transom — A horizontal bar of stone or wood across the opening of a doorway or window.

Trompe l'Oeil — A term referring to murals, usually painted on walls and ceilings as an architectural element, which attempt to disguise themselves through careful perspective and naturalistic use of color and form; literally, to "fool the eye." It was particularly popular as a device in Renaissance Italy.

Tympanum — The area between the lintel over a doorway and the arch above; often decorated, especially in churches.

Victorian — A style popular in the late 19th century which emphasized the polychromy and ornate decoration of the Victorian era in England.

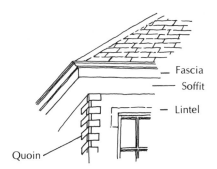

Fascia
Soffit
Lintel
Quoin

Pediment
Tympanum
Pilaster

Gratiam Habemus

Dennis Andersen, Curator, Graphic Materials, Richardson and Abbott Collection, University of Washington Libraries, Seattle, Washington

John Anderson, Chairman, Vegimal, Bristol, Vermont

Sylvia Arden, Head Librarian, San Diego Historical Society, San Diego, California

Bernard and Charlotte Atkin, Brooklyn Heights, New York

Victor Babel, Jr., Norwood, Massachusetts

Steven T. Baird, Architect, Salt Lake City, Utah

Steve Bajus, Head House Venture, Philadelphia, Pennsylvania

Rudy Barton, Cambridge, Massachusetts

Henry Beer, Communications Arts, Boulder, Colorado

Douglas A. Bennet, Shepley-Bullfinch, Cambridge, Massachusetts

Paul Bockelman, Cambridge Historical Commission, Cambridge, Massachusetts

Peter Brink, Executive Director, Galveston Historical Foundation, Galveston, Texas

Brent Brolin, Writer, New York, New York

Joseph Bruzga, Director, Neighborhood Revitalization Agency, Buffalo, New York

Beverly Bromley, Manager, The Landmarks Commission, Louisville, Kentucky

John K. Bullard, WHALE, New Bedford, Massachusetts

Robert Burley, Robert Burley Associates, Waitsfield, Vermont

Ralph Burstad, President, East Cambridge Savings Bank, Cambridge, Massachusetts

Donald Calarizo, Winchester, Massachusetts

Robert Campbell, Architect, Cambridge, Massachusetts

Dennis J. Carlone, Carlone & Associates, Cambridge, Massachusetts

Mimi Carter, Townscape Institute staff, Cambridge, Massachusetts

Mark Cassler, Owner, Cassler's Toy Store, Burlington, Vermont

Philip S. Chambers, Branch Operation Officer, Ladd & Bush Branch, United States National Bank, Salem, Oregon

J.A. Chewning, Architectural Historian, Cincinnatti, Ohio

Stephanie D. Churchill, Director, Utah Heritage Foundation, Salt Lake City, Utah

J.A. Citrin Sons Co., Detroit, Michigan

Barbara Clarke, Manager, Harold's Army/Navy, Corning, New York

Murray A. Cohen, Senior Construction Engineer, Cherry Hill, New Jersey

Roger Conover, Architectural Editor, MIT Press, Cambridge, Massachusetts

John Coolidge, Fogg Art Museum, Cambridge, Massachusetts

Jeffrey Corbin, Traverse City, Michigan

Diana Davis, Assistant to the Vice-President, Historic New Harmony, New Harmony, Indiana

Roberta Deering, Seattle, Washington

John H. Donnelly, Vice-President, Brown Insurance Agency, Montpelier, Vermont

Stanley Ehrman, Quick Quality Restaurants, New York, New York

Jean Elkington, Oregon Historical Society, Portland, Oregon

William Elwood, Professor, Charlottesville, Virginia

William Erlich, Cambridge, Massachusetts

Ruth Ferber, Jaques Ferber Furs, Philadelphia, Pennsylvania

George Fisher, Charles G. Hilgenhurst & Associates, Boston, Massachusetts

Linda Jo Fitz, Assistant Director, Foundation for San Francisco Architectural Heritage, San Francisco, California

Harry Fitzgerald, editor, *The Standard-Times,* New Bedford, Massachusetts

Susan Fleming, Artist, Salt Lake City, Utah

Edward D. Francis, Architect, Detroit, Michigan

Carl Franklin, McDonald's Corporation, Cherry Hill, New Jersey

Marilyn Frame, Manager, Cooper House, Santa Cruz, California

Noriko Fujinami, Studio Director, Venice, California

Gordon Fulton, Market Street Restoration Agency, Corning, New York

Ann Garret, Office Manager, Boston, Massachusetts

Paul Goldberger, Writer, New York, New York

Paul Goslin, Planner, City Hall, Portsmouth, New Hampshire

Paul G. Gosselin, Salmon Falls Associates, South Berwick, Maine

Roger Graham, President, J. Jessop & Sons, Jewelers, San Diego, California

James Groom, Robert Burley Associates, Waitsfield, Vermont

Eric Groves, Architect, Burlington, Vermont

Richard Haas, Artist, New York, New York

Laurie H. Halderman, Director of Publications, The Townscape Institute, Cambridge, Massachusetts

Arthur A. Hart, Writer, Salt Lake City, Utah

Anne Hasset, Landmarks Commission, Louisville, Kentucky

Thomas R. Hauck, Long Island University, Greenvale, New York

Thomas Hine, Writer, Philadelphia, Pennsylvania

Carter B. Horsley, Writer, New York, New York

Peter Jacobsen, Department of Historic Preservation, New Bedford, Massachusetts

Joseph Edwardus Jessop, Jeweler, San Diego, California

Peter Johnson, Designer, Cambridge, Massachusetts

Grant R. Jones, Architect, Seattle, Washington

Harvey Kaplan, Department of Planning and Community Development, Troy, New York

Margaret Kelleher, Librarian, Newburyport, Massachusetts

Faye Kephart, Market Street Restoration Agency, Corning, New York

William Kessler, Architect, Detroit, Michigan

George Kimball, Market Street Emporium, Portsmouth, New Hampshire

Patrick King, Photographer, Magna, Utah

Guernot Kuehn, Los Angeles, California

Richard Kugler, New Bedford, Massachusetts

John LaBranche, Curatorial Assistant, Strawbery Banke, Portsmouth, New Hampshire

Rollin R. LaFrance, Architect, Philadelphia, Pennsylvania

Phillip Langdon, *Buffalo Evening News*, Buffalo, New York

Laura M. Lane, Marketing Manager, Portland, Oregon

Jack Lawrence, Spirit of Venice, Venice, California

Chester Liebs, Historian, Burlington, Vermont

Catherine Lu, Planner, Arlington, Massachusetts

John Luton, Sr., First National Bank, Granbury, Texas

Adolf deRoy Mark, Architect, Carefree, Arizona

Sharon Marovich, President, Tuolumne County Historical Society, Sonora, California

Massachusetts Historic Commission, Boston, Massachusetts

Cynthia Matthews, Santa Cruz, California

David McCord, Boston, Massachusetts

Steve McHenry, The Button Factory, Portsmouth, New Hampshire

Peggi Medeiros, Office of Historic Preservation, New Bedford, Massachusetts

Janet T. Meunier, Research Historian, New Bedford, Massachusetts

Norman Mintz, Designer, Corning, New York

Ruth Mitchell, Bedford Stuyvesant Restoration Corporation, Brooklyn, New York

Arthur Cotton Moore, Architect, Washington, D.C.

Patricia Moore, Architect, Washington, D.C.

William Morgan, Professor, Louisville, Kentucky

Harriet Moyer, Center for Community Development & Design, Denver, Colorado

George E. Murray, Architect, Collge Park, Maryland

William S. Naito, Vice-President, Norcrest China Co., Portland, Oregon

Jeff Oberdorfer, Architect, Santa Cruz, California

Siobhan O'Neill, Museum Staff, Santa Cruz Historical Museum, Santa Cruz, California

James E. Palmer, Architect, San Francisco, California

Thomas Peet, Vice-President, First National Bank & Trust, Corning, New York

Charles Perella, Secretary-Treasurer, Economic Development Company of Lancaster County, Lancaster, Pennsylvania

David Piper, Manager, Leavitt and Peirce, Cambridge, Massachusetts

R. Jeffrey Points, Architect, Louisville, Kentucky

Jonathan Propp, Washington, D.C.

Gregory Ivanovich Ptucha, Board Coordinator, Pioneer Square Historic Preservation Board, Seattle, Washington

James Ragsdale, Writer, New Bedford, Massachusetts

Paul and Christine Rampon, Owners, Teddy's Lunch, Portsmouth, New Hampshire

Ronald T. Reed, Architect and Graphic Designer, The Townscape Institute, Cambridge, Massachusetts

Robert Rettig, Real Estate, Cambridge, Massachusetts

Anthony Robins, Landmarks Preservation Commission, New York, New York

Paula Robinson, Planner, Lancaster, Pennsylvania

Steve Rosenthal, Auburndale, Massachusetts

Terry Schoonhoven, Artist, Los Angeles, California

Alan and Tania Schwartz, Owners, Oasis Diner, Boulder, Colorado

Lee Schwartz, Photo Research, Philadelphia, Pennsylvania

Ralph Grayson Schwarz, President, Historic New Harmony, New Harmony, Indiana

Mike Semel, Chemung Engineering, Corning, New York

Al Shadel, Curator, Octagon Historical Museum, Santa Cruz, California

Laura Sharp, *The Standard Times*, New Bedford, Massachusetts

Linda Shea, Bank Manager, Venice, California

George Sheldon, Architect, Portland, Oregon

Michael Shreve, Seattle, Washington

Abner H. Silver, Owner, Jim's Steaks, Philadelphia, Pennsylvania

Penelope Simpson, Cambridge, Massachusetts

B.J. Smith, Owner, Brown's Cigar Store, Corning, New York

Melvin T. Smith, Preservation Officer, Salt Lake City, Utah

Tony Souza, Office of Historic Preservation, New Bedford, Massachusetts

Martha Stewart, Reference Librarian, Salt Lake City, Utah

Charles Sullivan, Director, Cambridge Historical Commission, Cambridge, Massachusetts

George Tesar, Senior Vice-President, Dayton Hudson Jewellers, Minneapolis, Minnesota

Arthur Tofani, Architect, Philadelphia, Pennsylvania

Noel Tyson, Architect, Philadelphia, Pennsylvania

United States National Bank, Ladd-Bush Branch, Salem, Oregon

James M. Vaughan, Director, Strawbery Banke, Portsmouth, New Hampshire

N.J. Walsh, Administrative Officer, Washington, D.C.

Raynor M. Warner, Architect, Boston, Massachusetts

Sam Waterhouse, Owner, Fowle's Drug Store, Newburyport, Massachusetts

Bob Weber, Philadelphia, Pennsylvania

Mary Webb, Townscape Intern, Belmont, Massachusetts

Evangeline Loes in Whorton, Research Vice-President, Galveston Historical Foundation, Galveston, Texas

Ted and Karene Will, Retailers, Fort Collins, Colorado

Sarah D. Williams, Brown University, Providence, Rhode Island

Winooski Community Development Corporation, Winooski, Vermont

Nore Winter, Architectural Planner, Downing/Leach, Boulder, Colorado

Jonathan J. Woodman, Architect, Newburyport, Massachusetts

Kenneth and Mary Zacks, Owners, Stewart-Zacks Fabrics, Traverse City, Michigan

Joan Zeenkov, San Diego Historical Society, San Diego, California

Selected Bibliography

Archetype, Spring 1982 (entire issue)

Berk, Emanuel. *Downtown Improvement Manual.* Chicago: The ASPO Press, 1976.

Blake, Peter. *Form Follows Fiasco: Why Modern Architecture Hasn't Worked.* Boston: Atlantic, 1977.

Blumenson, John J.G. *Identifying American Architecture.* Nashville: American Association for State and Local History, 1979.

Bonta, Juan Pablo. *Architecture and Its Interpretation.* New York: Rizzoli, 1979.

Brolin, Brent. *Architecture in Context: Fitting New Buildings With Old.* New York: Van Nostrand Reinhold, 1980.

Brolin, Brent. *The Failure of Modern Architecture.* New York: Van Nostrand Reinhold, 1980.

Brolin, Brent and Jean Richards. *Source Book of Architectural Ornament.* New York: Van Nostrand Reinhold 1982..

Connors, Joseph. *Borromini and the Roman Oratory.* Cambridge: MIT Press, 1980.

Cummings, Marcus F. *Architecture.* Troy: Young and Benson, 1865.

Cunningham, Bill. *Facades.* New York: Penguin, 1978.

Diamonstein, Barbaralee. *Buildings Reborn: New Uses, Old Places.* New York: Harper and Row, 1978.

Durand, J.N.L. *Précis des leçon l'architecture.* Paris, 1802.

Ewald, William R., Jr. *Street Graphics: A Concept and a System.* Washington, D.C.: The American Society of Landscape Architects.

Field, M. *City Architecture.* New York: Putnam, 1854.

Fleming, Ronald Lee. "Images of a Town," *Historic Preservation,* Oct. 1978.

Fleming, Ronald Lee/von Tscharner, Renata. *Place Makers: Public Art That Tells You Where You Are.* New York: Hastings House, 1981.

Graduate School of Design, Harvard University. *The Harvard Architecture Review: Beyond the Modern Movement,* Cambridge: MIT Press, 1980.

Greene, Herb. *Building to Last: Architecture as Ongoing Art.* New York: Architectural Book Publishing Co., 1981.

Hartmann, Robert R. *Design for the Business District.* Racine, Wisconsin: Racine Urban Aesthetics, 1979.

Haas, Richard. *An Architecture of Illusion.* New York: Rizzoli, 1981.

Hiller, Bevis. *Facade.* London: Mathews Miller Dunbar, 1976.

Hubbard, William. *Complicity and Conviction: Steps toward an Architecture of Convention.* Cambridge: MIT Press, 1980.

Huxtable, Ada Louise. *Kicked a Building Lately?* New York: Quadrangle, 1978.

Jencks, Charles. *Free-Style Classicism.* London: Architectural Design, 1980.

Jencks, Charles. *The Language of Post-Modern Architecture.* New York: Rizzoli, 1977.

Jencks, Charles. *Post-Modern Classicism.* London: Architectural Design, 1980.

Koetter, Fred. Interview in *Arcade.* March/April 1982.

Lynch, Kevin. *What Time is This Place?* Cambridge: MIT Press, 1972.

Mang, Karl and Eva. *New Shops.* New York: Architectural Publishing Company, 1982.

McCarthy, Bridget. *Architectural Crafts: a Handbook and a Catalog.* Seattle: Madrona Publishers, 1982.

Moore, Charles. *The Place of Houses.* New York: Holt, Rinehart, Winston, 1974.

Murray, Peter. *The Architecture of the Italian Renaissance.* New York: Schocken, 1963.

National Trust for Historic Preservation. *Old and New Architecture.* Washington, D.C.: Preservation Press, 1980.

Norberg-Schulz, Christian. *Genius Loci: Towards a Phenomenology of Architecture.* New York: Rizzoli, 1979.

Norberg-Schulz, Christian. *Meaning in Western Architecture.* New York: Rizzoli, 1980.

Portoghesi, Paolo. *After Modern Architecture.* New York: Rizzoli, 1980.

Pugin, Augustus W. *The True Principles of Pointed or Christian Architecture.* London: J. Weale, 1841.

Rifkind, Carole. *Main Street: The Face of Urban America.* New York: Harper and Row, 1977.

Ruskin, John. *The Seven Lamps of Architecture.* London: Unwin, 1903.

Safdie, Moshe. *Form & Purpose.* Boston, Houghton Mifflin Company, 1982.

Scrunton, Roger. *The Aesthetics of Architecture.* Princeton: Princeton University Press, 1979.

Sennett, Richard. *The Uses of Disorder: Personal Identity and City Life.* New York: Random House, 1970.

Smith, Peter F. *Architecture and the Human Dimension.* Westfield, N.J.: Eastview, 1980.

Stilgoe, John R. *Common Landscape of America, 1580 to 1845.* New Haven: Yale, 1982.

Sturges, W. Knight. *The Origins of Cast Iron Architecture in America.* New York: Da Capo Press, 1970.

Venice Biennale, *Architecture: The presence of the Past,* New York: Rizzoli, 1980.

Venturi, Robert. *Complexity and Contradiction in Architecture.* New York: Museum of Modern Art Papers on Architecture, 1966.

Venturi, Robert, Denise Scott Brown, and Steven Izenour. *Learning from Las Vegas.* Cambridge: MIT Press, 1972.

Vitruvius, *Ten Books of Architecture.* trans. by Morris H. Morgan. New York: Dover, 1960.

Von Eckhardt, Wolf. *Back to the Drawing Board: Planning Livable Cities.* Washington, D.C.: New Republic Books, 1978.

Photo Credits

FOREWORD

Courtesy of the Paola Chamber of Commerce, Paola, Kansas; Courtesy of George Bolster, Photography, Saratoga Springs, New York; Ronald Lee Fleming

INTRODUCTION

Courtesy of the Valentine Museum, Richmond, Virginia; Milo Stewart, courtesy of New York State Council on the Arts; Scala/Editorial Photocolor Archives; Scala/Editorial Photocolor Archives; Courtesy of the Rotch Library of Massachusetts Institute of Technology; Courtesy of the French Government Tourist Office; Courtesy of the Rotch Library of Massachusetts Institute of Technology; Courtesy of the Kansas State Historical Society; Ronald Lee Fleming; Courtesy of Oregon State Historical Society; U.S. National Bank—Ladd & Bush Branch, Salem, Oregon; Courtesy of Valentine Museum, Richmond, Virginia; Courtesy of Valentine Museum, Richmond, Virginia; Courtesy of Valentine Museum, Richmond, Virginia; Milo Foreman, Courtesy of New York Council on the Arts; Milo Foreman, Courtesy of New York Council on the Arts; Ronald T. Reed, The Townscape Institute; Courtesy of James & James, Portland, Oregon; Courtesy of Venturi, Rauch and Scott Brown; Ronald Lee Fleming; Rick Friedman; Bill Wippert, Courtesy of *Buffalo Evening News;* Ronald Lee Fleming

THE STORIES

I. Facade Survivors: Cambridge Historical Commission; Renata von Tscharner; Renata von Tscharner; San Diego Historical Society—Title Insurance and Trust Collection; Ronald Lee Fleming; San Diego Historical Society—Title Insurance and Trust Collection; Cambridge Historical Commission; Cambridge Historical Commission; Renata von Tscharner; Renata von Tscharner; Courtesy Gilder/Murray and Associates; Renata von Tscharner

II. Facades Restored: W.W. Dexter, *Picturesque Galveston,* 1900–1903, Courtesy Galveston Historical Foundation; Van C. Edwards, Courtesy Galveston Historical Foundation; Van C. Edwards, Courtesy Galveston Historical Foundation; Courtesy

Historic New Harmony, Inc.; Courtesy Historic New Harmony, Inc.; Courtesy Historic New Harmony, Inc.; Courtesy Historic New Harmony, Inc.; Courtesy Winooski Department of Community Development; Courtesy Winooski Department of Community Development; Courtesy Winooski Department of Community Development; Renata von Tscharner; Gary W. Cralle, Courtesy William R. Kessler Associates; Balthazar Korab, Courtesy William R. Kessler Associates; Courtesy Market Street Restoration Agency; Courtesy Market Street Restoration Agency; Kellogg Studio, Courtesy Market Street Restoration Agency; Kellogg Studio, Courtesy Market Street Restoration Agency; Staples-Herald Collection—Strawberry Banke, Inc.; Ronald Lee Fleming; Ronald Lee Fleming; Courtesy Jeffry Corbin Design; Courtesy Jeffry Corbin Design; Courtesy Jeffry Corbin Design

III. Facades Adapted: Gerald Ratto, Courtesy James A. Palmer, Architect; Gerald Ratto, Courtesy James A. Palmer, Architect; Courtesy Kentucky Landmarks Commission; Hugh Foshee, Courtesy Kentucky Landmarks Commission; Courtesy Arthur Cotton Moore/Associates; Courtesy Arthur Cotton Moore/Associates; Renata von Tscharner; Stevens Photo; Barber and Yergensen, Architects; Barber and Yergensen, Architects; Courtesy Santa Cruz County Historical Society; Cynthia Matthews; Cynthia Matthews; Nore V. Winter; Nore V. Winter; Sid Cohn—Historical Photography Collection, University of Washington Library; Courtesy Jones and Jones; Renata von Tscharner; Courtesy Galveston Historical Foundation; Courtesy Galveston Historical Foundation; Courtesy Cambridge Historical Commission; Steve Rosenthal, Courtesy Charles Hilgenhurst and Associates; Courtesy Cambridge Historical Commission

IV. Facades Reinterpreted: Renata von Tscharner; Renata von Tscharner; Jonathan Woodman Associates; Courtesy Adolf DeRoy Mark; Renata von Tscharner; Courtesy First Bank and Trust Company, Corning; Courtesy First Bank and Trust Company, Corning; Courtesy First Bank and Trust Company, Corning; Courtesy Abner H. Silver; Harold Joseph, Lee Schwartz Photo Research, Courtesy Abner H. Silver; Renata von Tscharner; Renata von Tscharner; Courtesy Henry Beer, Communication Arts; Nore V. Winter; Ronald Lee Fleming

V. Freestanding Facades: William Levy, Harper Realty; Ken Schroeder Associates; New Bedford *Standard Times;* Renata von Tscharner; Ronald Lee Fleming; Ed Hershberger; Courtesy Arthur Cotton Moore/Associates; Courtesy Arthur Cotton Moore/Associates; Norman McGrath, Courtesy Arthur Cotton Moore/Associates; Rollin R. LaFrance, Courtesy Mitchell/Giurgola Associates; Rollin R. LaFrance; Courtesy Mitchell/Giurgola Associates; Renata von Tscharner; Renata von Tscharner; Utah State Historical Society; Patrick King; Courtesy Steven Baird; Susan Fleming

VI. Lost Facades: Renata von Tscharner; Courtesy Galveston Historical Foundation; Security Pacific National Bank Photographic Collection/Los Angeles Public Library; Terry Schoonhoven; Terry Schoonhoven; Ronald Lee Fleming; Ronald Lee Fleming; Dennis Carlone; Dennis Carlone; Barry Hennings, Courtesy Tuolomne County Historical Society; Ronald Lee Fleming; Courtesy Oklahoma City Chamber of Commerce; Historic Preservation Office, Oklahoma Historical Society; Harriet Moyer; Frank Wing, Courtesy Foundation for San Francisco's Architectural Heritage; Rick Friedman; Rick Friedman

APPENDIX

Nore V. Winter, Nore V. Winter, Ron Reed, Nore V. Winter, Ronald Lee Fleming, Nore V. Winter, Ron Reed, Nore V. Winter, Nore V. Winter, Nore V. Winter, Nore V. Winter, Nore V. Winter, Ron Reed, Market Street Restoration Agency, Nore V. Winter, Nore V. Winter, Ronald Lee Fleming, Ronald Lee Fleming, Market Street Restoration Agency, Ronald Lee Fleming, Renata von Tscharner, Market Street Restoration Agency, Market Street Restoration Agency, Ronald Lee Fleming, Ronald Lee Fleming, Ronald Lee Fleming, Ronald Lee Fleming, Ronald Lee Fleming, Market Street Restoration Agency, Market Street Restoration Agency, Ronald Lee Fleming, Ronald Lee Fleming, Market Street Restoration Agency, Market Street Restoration Agency

PHOTO COLLAGE

All photos Ronald Lee Fleming and Renata von Tscharner

Index

125